Becoming Alec

Becoming Alec

A Novel

by Darwin S. Ward

MBM Press

Madison, WI

Becoming Alec
© 2007 Darwin S. Ward

First Edition

Published by
MBM Press
mbigmistake@gmail.com
www.darwinward.com/mbmpress

ISBN# 978-0-6151-7468-6

This novel is a work of fiction and no character is intended to portray any person or combination of persons living or dead.

Acknowledgments

Thanks to Dorie Clark and Don Schantz for their editorial help. More thanks to Dorie for giving me the notion that I could write a book. Further thanks to those who offered valued opinions on the manuscript, including BryGuy, Ninian, and Elsworth. Thanks to Jeff Muendel for logistical recommendations regarding publishing. And never said enough…thanks too for my sweetie's loving support and on-going super-human tolerance and capacity for forgiveness.

Cover: design by author,

layout by Michael Lemberger,

photo by Kael T. Block
(more of Kael's work can be found at http://xxboys.20six.fr/)

This book is dedicated to da boyz.

Chapter 1

Compared to the life she had known just a few years earlier as a homeless teenaged orphan in Chicago, being late to work should not have seemed like a big deal. But regardless, Alec nervously glanced at her watch and then peered through the window of the train door to see what stop she was at.

I'm never going to make it on time. The shift had run long at her apartment painting job and she had at least a 45 minute ride on the L to get to her evening dishwashing job back north of the loop. She had been able to balance the two jobs until just recently, when the deadline came down at the apartment building. Ruiz had told her that if she was late for work one more time that he'd fire her. Ruiz came from a long line of hard working Honduran immigrants. She had been able to charm him until now because she knew that he secretly liked her because she was a hard worker and didn't give him any crap or take smoke breaks like all of the other dishwashers. But this was the third time in two weeks and she knew that she was pushing it.

She got off the train and headed down the street at a brisk pace just short of a jog. In ten minutes she arrived at the restaurant a full hour and a half late for her shift. She bumped into Ruiz as she rushed to the time clock.

"Miss Alec, how nice of you to join us," Ruiz said.

Alec was exhausted from the rush and embarrassed for being late.

"I'm sorry, I know I'm really late. I'm just having a really hard time getting across town from my other job."

Ruiz didn't say anything, and let Alec clock in. Alec spent the rest of the shift waiting for the other shoe to drop. She didn't blame Ruiz for being frustrated with her, but she just couldn't manage to get to the restaurant on time sometimes.

After closing time, Ruiz approached Alec in the back room of the restaurant. She felt him walking towards her and her heart started to pound in her temple.

"You are hard worker, but I can't have you late all of the time. Who will wash the dishes from the late lunch crowd?" Ruiz said in his choppy English. "Besides, it look bad to the others. They think maybe they come in late too since Miss Alec come late all the time. This is a business. I have to look out for the business. I think maybe this doesn't work for us. I think you probably should find another place to come late to." Ruiz looked down at his feet and then away with regret. "I'm sorry, but it is for the business. We mail your last check to you. Tomorrow you don't come."

Alec took off her apron and clocked out and headed out the door back to the L. She hated getting fired. She was trying her best and it just wasn't enough, and getting fired made her feel a little like a failure at a job that ought to have been easy to keep. At the age of 20 and having supported herself with odd jobs since she was 14, Alec knew a thing or two about working hard and trying to keep jobs. She had done just about every low wage job in Chicago. In her younger days, some of those jobs she hadn't done so well. But she had worked hard for Ruiz. She should never have lost this one.

The next day at the apartment painting job Alec worried about having to look for another job and wondered how she could ever make a decent living.

"I'm working my ass off and I can barely make ends meet. What the hell am I supposed to do?" Alec asked a nearby coworker.

"That's the rub for us working stiffs," answered the coworker, Scott. "We do all the work and get none of the money. All the money goes to those snotty bastards who went to college on daddy's dime. It's the grand cycle of the American economy, and you and me are the sweat that keeps the gears moving."

Alec thought this conclusion a bit advanced considering Scott's normal bathroom humor level of conversation. "Geez, Scott, where'd you get that line of crap, from the Brotherhood of Carpenters and Joiners' bible?" Alec teased Scott.

"Very funny. But don't tell me I don't know which way the wind blows. At least you and me only got ourselves to feed. Poor Gary over there's got the wife and the yard apes." Scott began to holler so that Gary, who was standing a little ways away doing detailed edge painting work, could hear. "How do you do it, Gar, how do you bring home enough bacon for that crew of yours?"

Gary looked up from his work and walked over to where Scott and Alec were painting a wall together. "It's tough. I mean, I got this gig full time, not hourly like you guys, so that helps. And the wife takes care of the neighborhood kids for some extra money. Things are definitely tight, though."

Scott slapped Gary on the back and shook his head from side to side. "That's rough, man."

Gary continued, "The trick for folks like us that didn't go to college is to get into the trades. Not this lame painting crap, but you know, becoming a supervisor. A mason or a carpenter. Then you can make a decent wage. Then you can move up the ladder, or start working at custom sites. That's where all the money is." With that comment, Gary returned to his edge work.

Scott, not nearly as dedicated to his task, continued to commiserate with Alec. "Yeah, that's probably the way to go. Get some certification and start busting some balls like those fuckers that run this shop. Too bad you're a chick, you couldn't bust a ball if you tried."

Alec hated it when Scott gave her crap about being a woman. It was like an unfair dig. She couldn't help being a woman. Alec was well aware that, on more than one occasion, she had covered for Scott's sometimes shabby workmanship. Alec thought, too, that she was smarter than Scott, but she didn't hold it over his head. She wondered if her being a woman was the only thing that Scott could think of to give her crap about and thus make himself feel better.

She frowned at Scott and made a scoffing noise.

"Oh right, Scott, like you're such a ball buster. Yours are the first balls to bust when the supervisor comes in," Alec answered. Scott sneered in Alec's direction and made a motion ingrained from his Italian heritage with his hand against his chin.

That night Alec picked up a few papers on the way home from work and began looking for work to replace the dishwashing job. Though she lived very simply, in Chicago, even the shabby apartment that she had was pricey and she needed a second job to cover the costs. She scanned the papers for jobs that she could do in the evenings and that didn't require a high school or college degree. She had been lucky to avoid fast food work for the most part over the last several years, but she feared that she might have to take one of those sorts of jobs.

Amongst the papers was *The Windy City Times*, Chicago's gay weekly. She had picked it up mostly for fun, realizing that it wouldn't have many job listings. Depressed from the discouraging search, she picked up the *Times* for a break. After the catty advice column written by a drag queen, the pages and pages of photos taken of smiling pretty boys in bars, and the ads for phone sex lines, she found the small classified section. Her eyes were drawn to a small box on the page. "We Can Do It! Carpentry School for Women. Two Year program. Learn Valuable Skills to Start a New and Profitable Career. Get Paid While You Learn After Initial Three Month Classroom Period! Classes Start Sept. 1st."

Alec contemplated the ad. It sounded interesting. Two years of school, though. *Geez*. She hadn't been in school for almost seven years. They would probably balk at someone who didn't even have a high school diploma.

It was a Catch-22 for Alec. She felt like she couldn't get a decent job because she was a dropout. Without a high school diploma, she couldn't get a decent job, but she also didn't feel like she had the ability to go back to school either. And she wasn't even a high school dropout. She hadn't even managed to make it to high school. She couldn't support herself AND attend school. And she didn't even know, having left school at such an early age, if she could do well in a classroom setting ever again. Who would want an adult with only an 8th grade education in their classroom?

As she got off of the train she tossed the paper into a trashcan at the station.

Chapter 2

After several weeks of looking for work and going to interviews, Alec begrudgingly accepted a job at Kentucky Fried Chicken in the evenings to make ends meet.

Fast food was the ghetto of all jobs to Alec's mind. She wasn't above hard work, though, so she started the job with her head held high. Still, she figured that any job where your criminal background check was more important than if you had a high school diploma wasn't that promising.

Alec was hired to work the fry line. It was a simple, but hectic task and Alec often felt stressed out because her coworkers' incompetence and laziness tended to make the process harder than it had to be.

"I need two crispy breasts," Letitia, the 17 year old black girl who ran the cash register on the late shift called back to Alec.

"You should have two up there now," Alec called back.

"I used them a few minutes ago."

Alec sighed. *Of course you did. And of course you didn't bother to tell me that you did.* "I'll drop you two breasts, but it's gonna be awhile."

Letitia didn't bother to tell the customer what had happened. Instead she got herself a coke and went to go talk to a boy that she had a crush on who was sitting in a booth in the corner of the restaurant with some of his homies.

Things were generally slower after seven o'clock. It was harder to be sure that there was food ready for customers without much of it going to waste, and Alec hated when customers had to wait for food. Even though it was a lame job, Alec didn't see any need to do it poorly. At least working hard and doing a good job gave some purpose to being there.

The night manager, Les, who had a real Napoleon complex, emerged from the back room where he had been doing who knows what all evening, probably looking at porn on the internet.

Letitia heard the office door open and grabbed a nearby broom and pretended to be sweeping the dining room. The manager noticed that there was a customer waiting impatiently at the counter. "What can I do for you, sir?"

"I've been waiting for my chicken for over ten minutes," the irritated man answered.

Les turned to Alec. "Where's the man's chicken, Alec?"

"It's dropped sir, it will just be another minute or so."

Les frowned at Alec and sighed heavily. He turned back to the customer. "I'm very sorry sir. Can I offer you a free side dish?"

The customer perked up. "Yeah, give me some potatoes and gravy."

While Les filled a large side cup with potatoes, the alarm on the fryer beeped and Alec pulled the basket out of the grease and gave it a shake. Then she turned the basket over onto the draining area under the heat lamps. Without letting the chicken drain for the prescribed time, which made Alec wince, Les scooped the chicken up and completed the man's order. "Here you are sir, sorry about the wait. Come again."

The customer gathered the bag and left. Les went back to the fry line. "Alec, you've got to keep up with the orders. I can't be bailing you out every five minutes." Alec shot a look at Letitia, who was now back behind the counter innocently wiping it down with a rag. *That woman has done more cleaning in the last five minutes than she's done in the rest of her life.* Alec considered ratting on Letitia's shabby order work and obsession with the boys at the booth in the corner, but she decided that there wasn't any point.

"Yes sir," she said.

"I know that it's hard for you girls to get the hang of the fry line, so I try not to be too hard on you. Letitia's got the front though, so you'll just have to try a little harder back here."

"Yes sir," Alec parroted again. She wondered what he'd look like with a side of gravy poured over his bald head and a biscuit rammed up his ass.

Les smiled a self-satisfied smile that signaled that he was confident that he had gotten his point across. He headed back to his office. "Very nice with the cleaning," he said to Letitia in passing.

"Thank you Mr. Jones," Letitia said in a sickeningly sweet voice. As soon as Les closed the door to his office Letitia headed back to the boys' booth.

The fast food job left Alec feeling like she was covered in a thin film of grease each night. It was disgusting. And the people that she worked with, like Letitia, were lazy and, for the most part, slow on the uptake. This combination was infinitely frustrating to Alec, who was quick to learn new skills and who took great pride in her willingness to work hard. But she had no choice.

Alec began to wonder if her life would ever start to fall into place. It seemed like, no matter how hard she worked, she couldn't get ahead. To make matters worse, she was feeling lonely. When she had first moved to the City as a teenager, she had tried to break into social circles, but she felt awkward, like an outsider. Though she was young, she managed to get into the gay and lesbian bars, but those were hard places to meet people. From time to time she would answer a personal ad and date someone for awhile that she met that way. Those things never seemed to last, though.

These days she found that she was working so hard to make rent money that she didn't have time to look for love anymore. And the people that she met through the jobs that she was able to get as a high school dropout were hardly great friendship candidates. Besides, though she was smart, kind, and good-natured, she had always had trouble making strong connections with other people. She chalked it up to her shy nature.

And so Alec spent her days painting apartments in the sweltering summer heat and her evenings frying chicken in the artificial heat of the kitchen.

Alec and Scott ended up working together on the painting project for several months. Though she knew that Scott wasn't the smartest guy in the world, and that he had a tendency towards laziness, something about him amused Alec. The two of them teased each other or played little practical jokes on each other constantly. Alec wasn't used to enjoying the company of other people. She always had trouble making a good first impression and communicating with new people. Scott wasn't someone that Alec would ever consider a long-term friend, and she would never rely on him for anything, but he was just enough fun to be around to keep the days from being boring. She could be crude with Scott and he seemed to get a kick out of it, and Alec didn't give Scott a hard time for doing the same.

The other men at the job site tended to ignore Alec. The building trades were still a man's world. Aside from Scott, around most of the men Alec was quiet and kept her head down. She just tried to work hard and prove that she could hold her own.

One afternoon when Scott was off, a new guy at the apartment complex sidled up to Alec. "Hey there, I didn't know that they let ladies work here."

Alec glanced at the newcomer blankly and then returned to her work.

The new guy continued, "Seems like you'd fit in a lot better in my bedroom than here on a construction site."

Alec wasn't used to men treating her this way. For the most part men either befriended her or ignored her. She had never really had to worry about being propositioned and she was thrown off by the sleaze ball's directness.

After a moment to collect her thoughts she said, "You should probably back off buddy."

"Playing hard to get, eh? I can dig it," the guy said and retreated to his work.

A few hours later Alec was in a back section of the complex where the crew stored most of their equipment. She was cleaning brushes and putting things away for the shift. The new guy noticed that Alec was alone in the room and followed her in after a few minutes. He came up behind her, grabbed her wrists and turned her around. He pushed her up against a partially constructed wall and tried to kiss her.

Alec was about 5 foot 5 inches and relatively muscular for a woman. The guy was short for a man, maybe 5 foot 10 inches, and was thin. Alec probably out-weighed him. She flinched and turned her head so that he wasn't able to kiss her. Once she got her wits about her she was filled with rage tinged with fear. She kneed him in the groin and only managed to graze him because of her lack of leverage. The blow was enough to make him let go of her wrists to protect himself though.

"Hey, baby, don't be like that. I like a fighter, but no blows below the belt," he said as he began to approach her again.

Taking his advice, Alec promptly reared back and hit him squarely in the jaw, causing him to lose his balance and fall to the ground. Alec quickly left the room and rushed off of the worksite without even stopping to clock out for the day.

Alec got on the train and headed across town to KFC a little earlier than usual. Her mind was racing and her right hand was pounding. She looked down at it and saw that the knuckles were bloody and were beginning to swell. She felt at her hand and bent all of the fingers. Everything was sore, but there didn't seem to be any acute pain. She didn't think that she had broken anything, though she wasn't honestly sure how to tell. When she got to work she grabbed a cleaning towel and filled it with ice from the soda machine. She went out back behind the restaurant and sat in the alley with the packet of ice on her hand.

She marveled quietly at how, no matter how hard she tried, her life always seemed to kick her in the pants. It didn't matter where she worked or what she did, she just never seemed to fit in. She couldn't stand the thought of going back to that work site, but it was the best job that she had had in a long time. She didn't know what to do.

Alec worked her shift at KFC and headed home. On the train there was a copy of *The Windy City Times* lying on a seat. She picked it up and again saw the advertisement for the carpentry school for women. When she got home, she called the number for the school in the advertisement and left a message on the machine.

The next day a woman with a kind voice called her back and let her know that there were still positions left for the carpentry class that was to start in a few weeks. She explained the terms and the fees and agreed to send Alec an application and to arrange for tuition financing. Alec would have to scrape to get together the tuition money, but after a few months the program would begin to pay her a wage that was much better than what she was making at the restaurant. She had to take a chance.

Alec never went back to the apartment painting site and she tried to make the best out of the work at KFC, picking up extra shifts when she could over the following weeks.

Before she knew it, it was time for the first day of class. Alec got up early so that she would have time to get ready and make it on time for the 8am start. She got up, took a shower, and started a pot of coffee. She fumbled in a dresser drawer and produced a crumbled pack of Camels. She took out a cigarette and crawled through the apartment window out onto the fire escape and lit the cigarette. She didn't smoke often, but she was nervous and wanted to calm her nerves.

Maybe this whole idea was a big mistake. Maybe she really wasn't up to going to school. They would probably all think that she was stupid. She took a long drag on her cigarette. She turned and went back through the window to retrieve a cup of coffee, and as she went through the window frame, the window slid down and hit her in the head.

"Fuck!" It was about time she got out of this shit hole apartment. That settled it, she was going to try this school thing. Maybe it would turn out all right and she could finally start living a decent life.

Alec finished getting dressed and left to get on the train.

Chapter 3

The large wooden door had a frosted glass window with the words "We Can Do It Carpentry School for Women" painted in elegant black letters. Alec entered the office. There was a reception desk and a makeshift room divider behind it. On the other side of the divider Alec could see a room with about twenty chairs facing the back wall behind several long rectangular tables. At the back of the room there was a large white screen hanging from the ceiling with a projector and a computer set up to the side on a small desk. A door on the left side of the room seemed to lead into another space.

A handful of women were milling about the classroom. A heavy-set, but well-dressed middle-aged woman with long blond hair and long black eyelashes to match was sitting behind the reception desk.

"Hi honey, are you here for the first day of class?"

Alec smiled at the woman's warm approach in spite of her nervousness. "Yes, ma'am."

The woman smiled back at Alec and said, "Well, welcome. I'm Gail, I run the office here. If you ever need anything to do with paperwork or scheduling, you'll need to talk to me. Here's your first task, fill out these papers for me and I'll come collect them from everyone once class starts." Gail handed Alec a short stack of paperwork. "Now there's some coffee over there that you can help yourself to. Oh, and let's see, you'll need a nametag. What's your name, sweetie?"

"Alec."

Gail opened a marker and began to write, and then stopped.

"A-L-E-C?"

"Yes, ma'am," Alec answered.

"Oh, you are just so very polite. We'll get along just fine. But please do call me Gail. Ma'am makes me feel like your grandmother. I know that I'm old enough to be your grandmother, but I don't need to be reminded." Gail wrote Alec's name on a nametag in beautiful sweeping letters that matched the ones on the front door. Before giving Alec the nametag she looked on a list of names on her desk and placed a check next to Alec's name. Then she took the paper backing off of the nametag and gave it to Alec.

"Thank you Gail."

Alec went over to the small table where the coffee was and made herself a cup. Then she surveyed the other inhabitants of the room again. There was a large variety of women in the room. Tall, short, thin, fat, black, Hispanic, white, Asian, old, young. A true cross-section. More than half of them seemed like lesbians to Alec.

Alec walked to the other side of the room and took a peek into the open door. It contained a full carpentry shop with several workbenches set up around the periphery of the room all facing towards the center, where there was another station. Tools and electrical equipment seemed to hang from every available space on the wall. The room was clean, but there was a faint smell of sawdust.

Before Alec could start mingling with the other students, a thick woman with close cropped hair stepped to the front of the class and announced, "If everybody could take a seat and finish filling out your paperwork, we're gonna get started in about 10 or 15 minutes. So go ahead and finish up so that we can collect that before the lecture."

Alec picked a seat near the rear of the classroom and began filling out the paperwork. She finished up and then drank her coffee and observed the other students casually.

As was typically the case, none of the women seemed to take much interest in Alec. Alec was used to being the stoic observer, always just slightly off to the side of everything. To the straight women, Alec probably looked like an alien. The lesbians seemed to sense Alec's discomfort around people like dogs sense fear, so they kept to each other and left Alec alone.

After a while, Gail reappeared from the reception area and walked through the room collecting the papers from the students. When she got to Alec she smiled at her warmly again and said "Thank you, Alec."

Gail disappeared with the papers and attention focused on the thick woman, who was standing at the front of the class.

"All right, let's get started. Thank you all for getting here on time, I hope that is an indication of what I can expect in the future from this group. My name is Laura Smith, but no one calls me that but my mother. You all can call me Smitty, and then you'll fit right in. I am the President and CEO of this here women's school of carpentry. You all already met my better half, Gail, at the reception desk. She keeps this boat running smooth, so I suggest that you make friends with her early and you'll be much better off."

Gail peeked out from behind the room divider and waved, and Smitty blew her a kiss.

"So you are all here to learn to be carpenters. I've been working in this field since I was a kid, which was more than a few years ago. It always drove me crazy that there were never any other women doing carpentry. So, just about 14 years ago I decided to start this school. And Ms. Gail was kind enough to help me put all of the pieces together to make it happen. So here we are. There have been more than 500 women who have gone through this program and become carpenters. So we have a track record. If you work hard and pay attention, you'll do just fine and you can look forward to an interesting and lucrative career. I will certainly do everything that I personally can to assure that you succeed, but the rest of it is up to you.

"We'll spend three months here strictly in the shop, learning safety, basic carpentry techniques, and regulations. That's a full eight hour day, from 7am until 3pm, of classroom work. At the end of the three months, you'll be tested on what you have learned. If you pass, then, each of you will be matched up in the field with a professional carpenter to shadow that person's work and assist them. Once you get out in the field and begin shadowing a carpenter, you'll receive a wage of $30 per hour and you'll be eligible to join the union as a pre-apprentice. You'll shadow that first person until their job is finished, and then move on to shadow a new person. Every Friday we'll have you come back to the shop to do a day of additional classroom work on regulations and technique. If you stick with the program, at the end of two years you will be qualified to work in the field alone as a General Carpenter and you can apply to the union to get health insurance.

And then, if you want to, you can go on and get additional training in specific skills like drywall, floors, insulation, lathing, siding, concrete, or other various topics.

Someone raised their hand.

"Yes?"

"What happens if we don't pass the test at the end of the three months?"

"Ah, there's always an optimist in the crowd." The group let out a collective, nervous laugh. "If you don't pass we give you an opportunity to take the three month course over again at half of the original cost. And then you can take the test over again. If you can't pass after that then I would probably discourage you from being a carpenter. This job requires the ability to listen to instructions and to learn a variety of new things quickly."

For the rest of the session Smitty gave basic background on the wide range of work that carpenters do, outlined the basic regulations and certifications that govern carpenters, and took the students on a tour of the tools in the shop. Each student was given a list of supplies and safety equipment that they would need to acquire within a week.

By the end of the day Alec, as well as most of her 16 classmates, felt optimistic, but overwhelmed and brain-dead. She couldn't bear the thought of going to her job at KFC, but she knew that she had to keep working in order to be able to keep a roof over her head and still be able to pay for this program. Plus, she couldn't imagine looking for another job right now, especially one that would let her work her hours around the carpentry program. Besides, if she worked hard, in three short months she'd be working as an actual carpenter. She couldn't believe it. With an exhausted but happy heart, she left the school and headed to her job.

Alec's days soon became a blur of lectures and shop all day, sweating it out at the KFC all evening, and studying into the wee hours. She wanted to do well in the carpentry program so badly. She wanted to create a better life for herself, but it was a hectic pace. Most days she would go directly from class to work and stay there until after 10pm, which meant that she didn't get home until after 11. A quick shower and she would hit the books until she couldn't keep her eyes open anymore. Then she'd fall into a deep sleep, dreaming about carpentry regulations and different types of bevel cuts. She would wake up, inhale a bowl of cereal, and be out the door by 6:15am for another day. On weekends she would pick up extra shifts at KFC when she could to help pay for school.

Chapter 4

It was clear that Alec was a hard worker and was determined to do well in the program. It didn't take long for Smitty to notice Alec's effort. Smitty also noticed the polite respect that Alec paid to Gail each morning when she'd come into class and pass Gail's desk, no small thing considering many of the other women ignored Gail entirely. Smitty appreciated hard work, and she appreciated respect. More than anything else, Smitty appreciated Gail.

Smitty was a woman of strong character and a strong back. She was confident in the extreme. But Smitty owed all that she was and all that she had to Gail. Gail was her angel.

Gail was also as smart as a whip, and a whiz with finance and organization. She had spent her youth as an executive secretary, running offices for men who did not appreciate her. Similarly, Gail had spent her youth running a household for a husband who did not appreciate her. After raising her two children to adulthood, Gail realized that there was nothing bleaker than imagining spending the rest of her days with the lump that she knew as her husband. One day, not long after sending her second child off to college, Gail called in sick to her secretary job. She gathered together a carload of her things while her husband was at work. She went to the bank and withdrew one third of the family savings (figuring it only fair to leave money enough to pay for the house, which she intended to abandon to her husband). She got in her car and began to drive. When night fell, she found herself on the outskirts of Chicago. It wasn't long before Gail had set herself up with a new bank account, an apartment, and a new secretarial job.

A few years down the line, Gail's boss decided to renovate their office. A strong woman with a tool belt arrived at the office one morning and greeted Gail by saying, "Good morning, ma'am, I'm here to do the carpentry work if it won't trouble you too much." Over the weeks of the renovation Smitty and Gail flirted shamelessly, and it wasn't long before Smitty asked Gail out for dinner. Their relationship fell together easily. Gail had never considered herself a lesbian, or even given homosexuality a second thought. But she had rebuilt her life on the premise that she would never again be taken for granted and that she would never again settle for anything less than her own health and happiness. Smitty, an old-school butch dyke who came of age just before Stonewall, knew how to treat a woman well, and she treated Gail like a queen. In return, Gail smoothed out Smitty's rough spots and gave constant moral support to keep Smitty's ego afloat.

Gail could tell that Smitty hated working for men who didn't appreciate her as much as Gail had, and so, when Smitty began to talk about her dream to open a school to teach women the carpentry trade, Gail supported her wholeheartedly. Gail used her experience running an office and running a home to set up all the business particulars of the enterprise, and let Smitty handle the teaching. Now, so many years later, Gail and

Smitty were an inseparable team in perfect balance.

Smitty could see the determination in Alec's eyes. And Alec had Gail with that first "Yes ma'am." The evening after the first class Gail had hugged Smitty tight before going to bed and said, "You watch out for that Alec, she's a sassy little baby butch." And so it was quietly decided that Smitty and Gail would take Alec under their collective wing.

Chapter 5

Alec dutifully went to class each day and to KFC each night. Much to Alec's surprise, she enjoyed going to school, especially the hands-on work in the shop. Carpentry came easily to Alec and she learned new regulations and techniques quickly.

Alec sensed that the other students didn't quite know what to make of her. She was quiet and intent, focused on the tasks at hand. She was friendly enough when approached, but she rarely reached out to the other students.

The classroom had pretty quickly divided along the lines of sexual orientation. The half a dozen straight girls sat together on one side of the room while the lesbians inhabited the other half. Alec sat alone in the back, near a Puerto Rican woman whose orientation was as unclear as her English.

The group took a half hour lunch each day and most of them brought bag lunches because the shortness of the break didn't really allow for eating out. Alec would eat her peanut butter and jelly and listen to the other students talk to each other.

The straight women did crossword puzzles together over lunch, or brought in craft projects that they were working on to share with the group. Crochet or beading, mostly.

One day when Alec went to get her lunch from the refrigerator that Smitty and Gail had in the shop, she overheard a typical story.

"I came home and saw Larry out in the front yard brushing the dog. And would you believe, he was just letting the hair fly all over the yard. I tell you, it looked like it had snowed." One of the other women in the group gasped while still another stifled a giggle with her hand over her mouth. "I said, 'Are you out of your ever lovin' mind?' and all he could say was 'What? I mean, the very idea!" The woman shook her head from side to side. "He said I was yelling at him. I wasn't yelling. I just mean, what was he thinking?"

Normally, Alec wouldn't have said anything, but on this day she couldn't help herself. "It kinda sounds like you *were* yelling at him."

The group of women turned and all looked at Alec in shock. "I *wasn't* yelling at him."

Alec immediately realized that she should have kept her mouth shut. She shrugged her shoulders and threw her hands up in surrender. "Sorry, you're right." And she left the room.

This encounter, like so many other conversations that Alec overheard, made her sad. The women seemed so disconnected from their lovers and the men and women each seemed to have very little respect for each other.

The dykes, on the other hand, talked about their softball leagues or the carpentry work that they were trying out at home. There was one couple in the class in their early forties, who wanted eventually to start their own home improvement business together. The other seven lesbians ranged in age from their late twenties to their late thirties. Several of them seemed to know each other from outside the class. All of the dykes seemed sort of androgynous to Alec, and none of them were particularly attractive. In spite of this fact, several of them seemed to think quite a lot of themselves. Alec would hover around the edges of the group, but none of them seemed particularly interested in talking to her. She felt invisible. So after a while, she just focused on her studies.

Though she worried about it for weeks beforehand, Alec passed the three-month exam with flying colors.

Once the intensive classroom study was over, Alec was placed at a worksite in Schaumburg framing a new house under the observation of a forty-something carpenter named Jim. Jim was pleasant, but a no-nonsense sort who knew his trade well. Smitty's program provided carpenters like Jim with cheap, highly motivated and well-trained labor. Jim was happy to participate in the program, but mostly because of the benefits that it provided to him. Jim was reasonably good at explaining carpentry techniques, but he didn't go out of his way to mentor or befriend his apprentices.

Alec would rise early each day, before the morning rush hour, and put herself and her bicycle on the L headed to Schaumburg. She would take the train as far as she could, and then commute the last few miles on her bike with a large messenger bag slung over her shoulder to carry her tools and her lunch. She would work four 10-hour days, and then go to classes on Fridays. The compensation allowed her to quit her job at KFC, so, even though she was working long days, she suddenly found herself with more free time than she knew what to do with.

One Friday after class Smitty approached Alec. "Say, Alec, Gail and I were wondering if you might like to come over to our place some evening for dinner."

Alec was surprised. She looked up to Smitty. And she really enjoyed Gail's company just in the brief interactions that they'd had. She was unaware of the special interest Smitty and Gail had taken in her, though. Alec stuttered at first, but then said, "Sure, that'd be great."

"Super, do you have plans for tonight?"

"Nope."

"Great, then it's all set. We live on the north side, I'll go and write down the directions for you. Will you be driving or taking the train?"

"The train."

Alec wasn't accustomed to having dinner at people's houses, especially not at the home of two people who she deeply respected. She wasn't sure what to wear. Her wardrobe was littered with t-shirts, sweatshirts and jeans, mostly. She felt like the evening required something dressier, though. At the back of her closet she found a light blue button down long sleeve shirt and a pair of navy dress pants that she had from a stint as a waitress a few years back. The pants had a little bleach stain on the cuff, but she figured it was better than jeans.

Alec arrived at Smitty and Gail's modest bungalow on the north side around 6:45pm that evening. Outside winter was just starting to set in, but the house was filled with the delicious aroma of home cooking and Alec felt like the warmth from the kitchen drifted out to her and gave her a hug.

"Let me take your coat," Smitty offered.

Smitty hung Alec's coat and then led her into the combination kitchen and dining room.

"I hope that you like beef stew," Gail called out from her station at the stove.

"It smells great," Alec answered. Alec milled about the dining room, not quite sure what to say or what to do with herself. Smitty stood awkwardly across the table from Alec with her hands in her pockets. Finally, Smitty said, "Uh, you want a beer?"

"Yeah, thanks." Alec wasn't much of a drinker. She had only just turned 21 a few weeks earlier, but not having had parental supervision since puberty had left the door open to drinking at a younger age. It was an option that she hadn't often exercised, though. But Alec was glad that something had broken the silence in the room, so she was happy to accept a friendly beer. Smitty walked over to the refrigerator and produced two cans of Bud Light.

The three of them sat down to eat and Gail and Smitty took turns quizzing Alec about her life. It wasn't long before they got around to asking her about her dating status.

"Well, I've been so busy with school that I haven't had much time to date lately. I've dated off and on over the years, but nothing too serious," Alec said.

"Ah, you like to break those femmes' hearts," Smitty said knowingly.

"Well, I wouldn't really call any of my ex-girlfriends femmes per se. I mean, I don't think people really do that sort of thing anymore," Alec said.

Smitty nearly choked on her stew. "What do you mean people really don't do that sort of thing anymore?"

Alec avoided Smitty's eyes. She knew that she had offended her, but she couldn't help it if Smitty was living a lifestyle from the past. She didn't know how to recover from what she had said, though, and was afraid that she had just alienated two people who had been nicer to her than anyone else ever had been.

Gail stepped in to save everyone some face. "Now Smitty, don't get yourself hurt, maybe the child has never dated a femme before." And then Gail turned to Alec and gently put her hand on top of Alec's and spoke in a calm voice, "Sweetie, butch-femme is the highest and best expression of love and respect. Butch-femme is what heterosexuality tries to be, but fails. Lesbians take a dynamic about celebrating differences and inject feminist-style equality and respect. It is a truly beautiful thing, and it is a culture that is still very much alive today, even if you've not yet been part of it." Gail squeezed Alec's hand and then gave a loving look in Smitty's direction. Smitty's anger melted away under Gail's gaze.

Smitty added, "A butch takes pride in protecting and respecting her femme. A femme takes pride in caring for her butch and being as beautiful for her as she can."

"And femmes make sure that their butches don't let their passion get the best of them," Gail said with a wink that nearly made Smitty blush.

Smitty continued, "How you could have gotten this far in life without knowing that you were a butch I can't understand."

Alec was taken aback. "What do you mean? I'm not a butch."

"Well, you're definitely not a femme, that's for sure." Smitty countered.

Gail intervened again. "Honey, it's just that you really do seem like a butch. You're just such a gentleman about everything, and you have the cutest little butch haircut."

Now Alec was the one who blushed.

Gail continued, "Maybe, just maybe, if you met a femme who knew how to take care of you, you might find that you liked it and that you would find a family in our circle of society. There is a lot of pride in butch-femme culture. Our sisters were there in those bars in the pre-Stonewall years when it wasn't okay to be gay. They paved the way for all of the freedom that we all enjoy today."

Alec nodded in understanding.

The conversation moved on to other topics. Gail brought out a cake that she had baked and Alec enjoyed two large pieces. Soon, it was late and Alec made her way home on the train as a light snow began to fall.

Chapter 6

As winter blew over the Windy City, Alec began to settle into work and become more confident with her carpentry skills. She started having regular Sunday meals at Gail and Smitty's place. They were the closest thing to family that she had had for a very long time. In many ways, they were the first decent type of family that she had ever had. The more time that she spent with Smitty and Gail, the more that she learned about butch-femme relationships. Alec began to wonder if they were right and that she really was a butch.

Alec's job with Jim wrapped up one week in mid-January, and after class that Friday Alec decided to go out on the town to celebrate the end of her first carpentry project. On Monday she would start anew with a different mentor on a different project.

Alec got home from class, cleaned up the apartment, and made dinner. She took a shower and got on her sharpest, butchest looking clothes and splashed men's cologne generously on her body. Then she headed out to

Andersonville to hit one of the lesbian bars there.

Alec had more free time now that she wasn't trying to work multiple jobs, but she found that she was physically and mentally exhausted in the evenings, and she still had studying to do, so she had not been out to a club for quite a while. She stopped in to Club 69, a place where she often hung out in her late teen years with her fake id, but that she hadn't been back to in years.

Alec sat at the bar and drank a Miller Lite and surveyed the crowd. It was still relatively early. She went to the entryway and grabbed *The Windy City Times* and returned to her stool to read. Time passed and the club began to fill up with women chatting excitedly.

Alec finished the paper and set it down and scanned the crowd again. Her eyes settled on a group of three women sitting in a booth in the corner. They were drinking cocktails and laughing frequently. One of the women had short dark hair teased up with styling gel to spiky peaks. She had several earrings up the side of her right ear and a diamond stud in her nose. She had her arm around a woman to her left who had long, straight blond hair and was wearing a mini skirt and a mesh top. The woman on her left had curly reddish-blond hair that hung down just to her shoulders. She wore a delicate white, lacy sweater over a camisole that peeked out from just under the sweater and tight blue jeans. As Alec observed the trio, the woman with the curly hair glanced in Alec's direction and they made eye contact for an instant.

Alec felt a little charge go through her body. The woman returned to her conversation with her friends, but Alec continued to watch her. She was very pretty in an easy, unpretentious way. She didn't seem to be trying to show off nearly as much as her two friends. She was very feminine in a natural way. She had a quiet confidence in her manner that was alluring.

Alec could grasp from the scene that the other two women were in a couple, quite obviously a butch-femme couple, which left the possibility that the beautiful stranger might be single.

A cocktail waitress came up and stood at the service station at the bar next to Alec waiting for the bartender to finish what she was doing and take her order. "Say, could you send a drink to someone for me?" Alec asked the waitress.

"Sure, no problem, who are we talking about?"

"The curly-headed blond at that table in the corner, " Alec answered.

"Oh. Jessie. Nice choice. What should I send her, what she's already drinking?"

"Yeah, that sounds good," Alec said. "So her name's Jessie?"

"Yup. And you owe me $3.50. Oh, say, do you want her to know who sent the drink?"

"Yeah." Alec paid the waitress and waited for her to gather her orders at the bar and distribute them throughout the room. After about ten minutes she finally deposited the cocktail at Jessie's table. The waitress leaned in and said something to Jessie, and then they both turned around and looked in Alec's direction. Alec lifted her head ever so slightly to identify herself. Jessie took the drink and continued to talk and laugh with her friends.

Alec turned back around to face the bar and slowly drank her beer. After an excruciating ten minutes, she felt a finger tap her on the shoulder. It was Jessie.

"Thanks for the drink. It's my favorite. How did you know?" Jessie said.

"Lucky guess," Alec lied. "I'm Alec."

"Jessie. So Alec, do you make it a habit of picking up women in bars?"

"Only the really pretty ones," Alec said, trying to be cool.

"Good answer."

Alec and Jessie chatted and flirted for a while at the bar, and then Jessie invited Alec to join her and her friends at the table. The friends talked at Alec, but she answered their questions without paying them much attention. She was mesmerized by Jessie.

Eventually, Jessie's friends excused themselves, seeming to realize that they were only intruding. Jessie and Alec talked easily long into the evening. It seemed like no time passed at all before the lights at the bar were coming up to announce closing.

Alec knew that she could ask Jessie to come home with her and that she had a good chance, but she liked Jessie too much, and she was overcome by an unexpected desire to take things slow. They left the bar and Alec walked Jessie, who only lived a few blocks away, home. Jessie gazed into Alec's eyes as they stood on her front stoop together and Alec wondered what she was thinking.

Eventually, Jessie dug in her purse for a pen and a scrap of paper. Finding no paper, she took Alec's hand and wrote her phone number down on Alec's palm. The pen tickled Alec's skin and a little charge went through her body. Alec took the phone number as a good sign that Jessie liked her too.

Alec leaned forward and gave Jessie a bear hug. As she began to let go, Jessie leaned in and gave Alec a long, gentle kiss on the lips. They paused and looked into each other's eyes, and then kissed again, this time exchanging tongues. Alec sighed and squeezed Jessie again and then said goodnight and walked off into the darkness towards the L station.

The next Sunday at Smitty and Gail's place Alec could hardly contain herself. Smitty sat on the couch and watched *60 Minutes* while Gail watched over the potato leek soup on the stove. Alec set the table for Gail and put away the dishes from the drying rack.

"Thanks sweetie. I think we're ready. Why don't you go retrieve Smitty?" Gail said.

The three of them sat down together to eat. Smitty noticed an uncharacteristic grin on Alec's face. "What are you smiling at, monkey?" she asked.

"Oh, nothing," Alec said, trying to seem nonchalant.

Smitty and Gail shot each other a knowing look.

"Nothing, huh? Well, don't expect me to beg for details," Smitty said.

Another moment passed and Alec couldn't bear it any longer. "I met somebody."

"Oh honey, that's great," Gail said. She put her hand on Alec's hand and gave it a squeeze.

"Met somebody, huh?" Smitty said with mock skepticism. "So who is this woman?"

"Her name's Jessie. I met her at the club."

"What's she like?" Gail asked.

"She's beautiful. She has curly reddish-blond hair. And she's nice and smart and fun."

"Long hair?" Smitty asked.

"Oh Smitty, give the girl a break," Gail said.

"Yeah," Alec said, "she's a femme."

"Well it's about time," Smitty said as she winked at Alec and slapped her on the back.

Chapter 7

Over the following weeks Alec and Jessie were inseparable. They stayed up until late, late in the evenings talking about everything under the sun. They went to movies and out to dinner and on long walks. And it wasn't long before they gave in and consummated their relationship.

As the weeks turned into months it became clear that the travel between Alec's ratty apartment downtown and Jessie's nicer place in Andersonville was not worth the inconvenience. And the longer that they dated, the more often that they spent time exclusively at Jessie's place. When Jessie asked Alec if she would move in with her, Alec didn't hesitate. Besides wanting to be with Jessie all the time, Alec was relieved finally to be rid of her old place and was happy to have someone tolerable to share rent with.

Alec thought Andersonville was a nice neighborhood. Originally inhabited by Swedish immigrants, the area had long since been taken over by Hispanics and lesbians. The neighborhood had an eclectic mix of bakeries, small shops, gay bars and nightclubs, the Swedish American Museum, quaint bookstores, restaurants, and some of the best coffee cake outside of Sweden. Jessie lived in an apartment a few blocks off of Clark, well within walking distance of the red line train stops and several great restaurants and bars.

Jessie was Alec's first serious relationship and Alec was very happy to be with her. They got along easily and living together was no problem. Alec thought, now that she was on her way to getting a good career and she had a wonderful girlfriend, that she ought to feel complete.

But just as had been the case her entire life, something didn't feel quite right. She tried to talk to Smitty about her uneasy feeling a few times, but Smitty was convinced that Alec just had to grow into and accept her new butch identity. Alec began to feel like she must be crazy not to be happy now that her life was finally falling into place. She had worked so hard to get where she was, she didn't understand why everything wasn't perfect now.

Alec wasn't accustomed to having to deal with complex emotions. Most of her life she had lived hand to mouth and reflecting on life was a luxury that she just hadn't had. She also hadn't had the luxury of friends to talk to about her problems. Being surrounded by loving people meant that, when she was down or moody, she had to figure out a way to communicate a reason why to those people, so that they wouldn't think that she was mad at them. Alec wasn't sure how to accomplish this. She empathized with others easily, but she didn't know how to express her own emotions very well. This simultaneously made her feel like her feelings were bottled up and also like others were pressuring her for emotional reassurance that she wasn't sure how to give.

She began to worry more and more often about these feelings, beginning to wonder if she was crazy or just doomed never truly to be happy.

One night the pressure in Alec's head got to be too much. She broke down crying in bed. Jessie heard Alec's weeping.

"What's wrong, baby?" Jessie asked sleepily. She had never known Alec to cry.

Alec continued to weep quietly for several moments.

"Talk to me, honey."

Alec choked back tears and began to speak. "I don't know what's wrong. It just feels like, no matter what I do in my life, I don't feel right. I don't seem to fit in. I'm so happy with doing carpentry and with being with you, but inside things still feel unsettled. I feel like I must be crazy or something."

"It's okay, sweetie, sometimes we all feel that way."

"But, sometimes it's hard to get up every day and go on. There's like this unbearable weight on my back."

Jessie prodded Alec, but Alec wasn't able to articulate her feelings any further. After many long hours of·talking, Jessie convinced Alec that, if something felt so terribly wrong, that maybe she should go to see a therapist.

The next day Alec's resolve weakened, though. She felt foolish. She didn't want to spend the money that therapy would require and she wasn't sure that therapy could help her. She wanted to be able to solve her own problems.

Alec continued working each day and going to classes on Fridays. She and Jessie went to dinner each Sunday night at Smitty and Gail's place. Alec's money troubles began to get better and she wasn't having to work nearly so hard. Nothing was wrong, but she started to have more and more of a nagging feeling of unease. She felt moody and isolated, even though Jessie was loving and kind.

Alec tried to pinpoint what the problem was, but it was hard. It felt like, for the first time in her life she wasn't just trying to survive from moment to moment. But instead of feeling relief, she felt nervous. Suddenly she had time and energy and she found that her mind began to drift dangerously.

Her entire life Alec had felt strange. Different. Alone. When she was young, she thought this sense of feeling different was because she felt attracted to women. After she got kicked out of her parent's house and moved to Chicago, she thought that she felt different because she didn't have a high school diploma like everyone else and she didn't have a family like everyone else. When she met Smitty, she hoped that the discovery of butch-femme culture would finally make her feel like she belonged somewhere. Nothing seemed to help, though. She still felt isolated.

Alec knew that Jessie was worried about her. One morning Alec got up and was getting ready to go to work when she spotted a $100 bill on the kitchen table with a note that had a phone number on it and the simple words,

Dr. Taffe is a gay positive therapist. I love you, please go.

Chapter 8

Alec entered the lobby of the building. The furniture had been updated, but the architecture was a dead giveaway that the building had been built in the 1960s. Alec walked down a long gray-green lit hallway until she found suite 110. Innocuous letters on the door spelt out, "The Midwest Center for Human Services." It sounded like an HR firm. Or an escort service.

Alec entered the office and glanced around the room nervously. It seemed that the missing 1960s furniture from the lobby had found its home here. On the wall a large plastic display case held paper pamphlets with titles like, *So you think you have an eating disorder...* and *Sobriety Starts with You*. On a small table in the corner there were 6-month-old issues of *Time* and *People* interspersed with several copies of *Highlights for Children*. In one of the 1960s chairs there was a clipboard with a pen. On top of a pile of papers was a note that read, "Alec".

Alec picked up the clipboard and sat in the chair where she had found it. She began looking through the paperwork and filling in blanks.

Name. Address. Gender. *Weird.* Under gender there were more than just two choices. There was a third blank next to transgender/transsexual. This place really WAS progressive. Medical history. Family medical history. Shit, she didn't know anything about her family medical history. Patient's bill of rights. Geez there was a lot of stuff to fill out. Insurance. *Ha.*

Alec filled in as many of the blanks as she could and then set the clipboard down on a side table next to her chair. She looked at the 1960s clock on the wall. *Three oh one.* She looked at her watch. *Three oh six.* Hmmm. A few moments passed. She looked at her watch again. *Three oh eight.* She started to wonder if this was the right office. If this was the right time and day. Of course, there was the clipboard. Hmmm. Watch. *Three ten.* Wall clock. *Three oh five. Shit. Come get me already.* Maybe she should go look for someone. Maybe they forgot about her appointment.

"Alec Jensen."

A short, sharply dressed woman with perfect hair and makeup suddenly appeared in the doorway, her voice seemingly preceding her presence.

Alec jumped to her feet with a start and smiled at the woman weakly.

"How are you? I'm Dr. Jantina Taffe. Come on in." Dr. Taffe motioned for Alec to enter the doorway.

Alec went with Dr. Taffe down a short hall to a small, sparsely decorated office. There was a maroon colored couch, much more modern than the furniture in the waiting room, a desk, a large overstuffed leather chair, and a bookcase filled to the brim with books. Several framed degrees hung on the wall. A Tiffany style lamp cast a warm glow over the room.

"Have a seat," Dr. Taffe said as she motioned to the couch.

Ah, the shrink's couch.

"Can I get you something to drink? Water? Tea?"

"No," Alec said, "I'm fine," even though her throat was dry.

"So," Dr. Taffe began as she settled into the big leather chair, "what brings you to see me?"

"Well," Alec began tentatively. She looked down at her hands. She had been biting her nails and one of her cuticles was bleeding a little bit. She hoped that she didn't bleed on the nice couch.

"It's okay, take your time," Dr. Taffe said.

"I've never been to therapy before. I don't know what to say," Alec said.

"Was there something that happened that made you want to make this appointment?"

"Uh, not really. I mean, I'm not sure. I just don't feel right."

"Is this a recent feeling?"

"Uh, no."

"How long have you felt like things weren't right?"

Alec paused. She felt stupid. "Uh...I think that I've always felt that way."

Dr. Taffe paused and made a note on the pad on her lap. "Okay. Is there something specific that you feel isn't right, or is it just a general sense?"

"It's kind of a general sense."

"Are there things in your life that do seem to feel right?"

"Yeah, I mean, sort of. I have a great girlfriend. And I'm in this cool program where I'm learning to be a carpenter and I like that. They even pay me to learn, which is cool. And I like the people in the program, especially the lady that runs it."

"That sounds like you have several things that you feel good about," Dr. Taffe said.

"Yeah."

Dr. Taffe paused and smiled at Alec, gently waiting to see if Alec would add more. After an uncomfortably lengthy silence, she continued. "So do you have some idea what it is that doesn't feel right?"

"No, not really."

"Why don't you tell me about your life? Why don't you give me your history so that I can learn more about you?" Dr. Taffe said.

Alec had spent a long time trying to forget everything that had happened to her before she came to Chicago and she wasn't thrilled with the prospect of having to recount it for Dr. Taffe.

"Like, from the beginning?"

"Yes. I think that would be helpful for both of us if you don't mind." Dr. Taffe smiled warmly.

"Ok. Well. I grew up in Belleville, you know, northwest of the city. My dad worked at the assembly plant. My mom did some waitressing, but she seemed to have trouble keeping a job."

"Why was that?"

"I don't know. She was out of it a lot. She had a back problem that she took a lot of medicine for. She was just kind of flaky."

Dr. Taffe nodded and wrote some notes on her pad.

Alec couldn't remember when she had lost respect for her mother. It just seemed like her mother was never *there*. Physically, she was around, but mentally she was just *gone*. Alec had learned at an early age just never to rely on the woman for anything. She learned to forge her mother's signature on school forms. She also learned to make excuses for her mom both at school and when her mom's bosses would call. "My mom can't come to the open house, she's visiting her sister in Michigan." "Helen can't come in to work today, she twisted her ankle gardening this weekend." Meanwhile her mom would be home asleep, or doped up and incoherent on pain killers and booze.

Alec continued. "Anyway. Dad worked a lot, so he wasn't around much."

"Are you the only child?"

"Yeah."

"So your father worked a lot. Did you get along with him?"

"Um. Dad was pretty strict. He didn't take any shit."

"What do you mean?"

"I had to be pretty careful what I would say to him."

"What would happen if you weren't careful what you said?"

Alec paused, considering her words. "He'd get mad."

"How would you know he was mad? Would he yell at you?"

"Yeah. He yelled a lot. Sometimes if I was being a jerk he might smack me."

"He would hit you?"

"Sometimes. Not very often."

"Did he hit your mother too?"

"Yeah."

"Did your mother ever do anything about getting hit? Did she ever leave him?"

"No. She just kind of took it. Like I said, she was sort of a flake."

"Besides the yelling and the hitting, was there anything else going on that made you uncomfortable."

"No. I mean, if you're asking if he molested me, no, he would never do that. He was a good guy. He just lost his temper sometimes. Sometimes I deserved it."

"Somehow I doubt that you deserved to be physically abused, no matter how bratty that you thought you were behaving."

"Yeah. I guess." Alec shifted nervously in her seat.

Alec never thought it was odd that her father hit her. She *really* never thought it odd that he hit her mother. Sometimes she felt like shaking her mother violently herself. She knew that her dad was just trying hard to hold things together. He would work all day and then have to deal with her mother's bullshit. Or her mother would lose another job and her dad would have to take double shifts to make ends meet. Alec didn't blame him for being mad. He was a strong man, a proud man. Alec felt bad that she hadn't matched up to his standards.

"Go on with your story."

"So, yeah. I kinda started figuring out that I might be gay when I was maybe, ten. I was always a tomboy. Ya know, my friends were all guys in the neighborhood. When we started to get older they kinda stopped hanging out with me. I kinda had a hard time making friends with the girls. The girls at my schools always seemed really snobby and stuck up. So I had a hard time getting along with them."

"So most of your friends were boys?"

"Yeah. At least until middle school. After that the boys didn't want to talk to me anymore."

"So after middle school who did you hang out with?"

"Nobody, really. I just kind of spent a lot of time alone. I didn't really feel like I fit in anywhere. That's kind of what I mean about things not feeling right."

"Okay." Dr. Taffe took some notes.

"Besides, the kids at school were idiots."

"Were they mean to you?"

"They would give me a hard time. I don't know how, but it seemed like everybody knew I was a dyke. It's not like I was dating anybody or anything. And I didn't tell anybody. But everyone knew. So kids would call me dyke all the time and spread rumors about me."

"That must have been hard."

"Yeah. I didn't care." Alec's voice seemed tough, but her facial expression belied that she really did care. "Except then, this one night, some kids came to my house and wrapped it with toilet paper and threw eggs at it and they spray painted the garage door with the word dyke."

Alec had become aware of sex when she was about eleven. She started having these reoccurring dreams about the singer Sheryl Crow. She kept having these dreams that she was being breast fed by Crow. Not as a baby, either, but as the age that she was. She thought it was pretty weird at the time, but she figured that it meant something besides what it seemed like.

Within a year she was starting to have sexual fantasies about her classmates. It was always about the prettiest girls in her class or in the class a year ahead of her, girls who would have never even given her the time of day. She used to imagine taking them into the girl's bathroom between classes and performing oral sex on them.

"What did your parents do about the vandalism incident?"

"They freaked out. My dad asked me if I was a 'fucking sicko dyke' and I told him that I didn't know. So he kicked me out of the house. He didn't even let me take anything with me, really. Except my bicycle, I took my bike."

"How old were you?"

"Fourteen. I was just about to finish eighth grade."

"So what did you do?"

"I spent the night in a park a couple of nights. And then I figured that there was no reason to hang around. So I started riding my bike to Chicago. It took me a couple of days. But I got here. I've been here ever since."

"Wow, that's quite a journey for a young girl."

"It wasn't that big of a deal." Alec looked down at her hands.

"So what happened once you got to Chicago?"

"I slept in parks for a while. I got a job as a dishwasher at a restaurant pretty quickly. The lady at the restaurant was really nice to me. She would let me eat for free. Then I got another job cleaning hotel rooms. When it got colder I started renting rooms at the hotel to stay in. Eventually I got enough money to rent a room in an apartment with a couple of other people. I saw it in the paper. They were freaks, though, drug addicts. So I tried to work as much as possible so that I could get out of there. I really wanted a place on my own, but it's expensive in Chicago, so it took a long time. I've had a lot of jobs in this town."

Alec had done the best that she could when she arrived in Chicago. Money was tight and she was very young, but she grew up fast. She was lucky that nothing really horrible had ever happened to her. She was lucky too that she had enough pride and self-awareness that she didn't let herself slip into drug or alcohol abuse. The image of her mother, passed out in the middle of the day, helped her stay clean too.

Besides making enough money to keep a roof over her head, Alec spent most of her time in the early days in Chicago trying to lose her virginity. Jailbait wasn't exactly the most appealing selection at the gay and lesbian bars in Chicago, though. Alec didn't have access to the internet or even really know how to use a computer yet, so she had a hard time finding other gay people. Eventually, she started answering personal ads in *The Windy City Times*. She lied about her age to the people that she met through the ads, and she was able to have a string of short-lived relationships that way. The personal ads never seemed to pan out to a long-term relationship, though, and Alec had wondered what it would be like to be in love. Meeting Jessie was pretty spectacular.

"Where are you living now?"

"Well, I was living in this shit hole near Lincoln Park for a long time, but I moved in with my girlfriend in Andersonville this last spring."

"How's that going?"

"Pretty good. I like her a lot."

"And now you're in the carpentry program?"

"Yeah, I really love that."

"That's great."

A moment of silence passed in the room.

"Well, Alec, that's about it for today. I'd really like to see you again, though. Do you think we could set up a time next week?"

"Um. It's kind of expensive."

Dr. Taffe glanced at her notes. "You don't have insurance?"

"Nope. I won't get insurance until after my apprenticeship is finished."

"Well, that's not a problem. We can do a sliding scale. My rate starts at $75. Do you think that you could swing that?"

"Not every week."

"How about we set a time for two weeks from now and see how it goes after that? We have some funds to help folks who can't pay, so I can look into that and see if there is any money available."

"Okay."

Alec and Dr. Taffe arranged to meet again in a few weeks and Alec left the office and headed back to the apartment.

Chapter 9

Alec had a sense like she was a bottle full of carbonated beverage that someone had shaken up. The only problem was, she couldn't get her cap off to release the pressure. She wondered if going to see the therapist was really worth the money, even if it was heavily subsidized by the clinic charity fund. After the first visit, she didn't feel any better. Seeing the therapist hadn't released the pressure building in her head, it had only reminded her of several things in her past that she'd just as soon forget about.

The two weeks passed quickly and it wasn't long before Alec found herself sitting in the 1960s waiting room again.

"Last time you gave me some history about your life. Thank you for doing that. Today I'd like to try and pinpoint a little bit better just what it is that is troubling you," Dr. Taffe said.

"Okay."

"You said last time that you 'don't feel right'. I'd like to find out what that means to you."

Alec nodded.

"When you think about not feeling right, what words come into your mind?"

Alec sat and thought for a few minutes. "Confused."

"Good. What else?"

"Awkward. Weird. Different." Alec paused. "Alone."

"Okay. Good. Do you have some sense of what it is that feels 'different'? Or, to think about it another way, what do you feel 'different' from?" Dr. Taffe asked.

"Different from everyone else."

"Is there anyone that you DON'T feel different from?"

"Not really."

"Has there EVER been anyone that you didn't feel different from?"

Alec thought for a minute. "Well, I guess that, when I was little and I used to play in the neighborhood, I felt pretty normal then."

"This was when you used to play with the little boys in the neighborhood?"

"Yeah."

"What sorts of things did you do together back then?"

"I don't know. We just played kid's games."

"Like what?"

"You know, football...baseball...kickball. Sometimes we would play this spy game where we would hide from each other and then hunt each other down with toy guns or water balloons. Or we would play with action figures or little toy cars. We rode our bikes around the neighborhood and jumped them off of ditches or homemade ramps. Just normal kid stuff."

"Were you always the only girl, or were there other girls from the neighborhood who would play with your friends?"

"No, I was the only girl. They all liked me though. They never treated me like a girl. And I guess I didn't feel like a girl."

"They didn't make you play 'girl parts' when you would make believe?"

"No. There weren't any 'girl parts'" Alec said and she furrowed her brow, not really understanding why the doctor was asking her about ancient history that didn't seem to matter.

"So that was a situation where you felt normal?"

"Yeah. I never really thought about it before, but yeah, I felt pretty normal back then."

Dr. Taffe wrote some notes down.

"Alec, let me ask you something else. When you think about yourself, what makes you feel most 'not right'?"

"I don't know, just everything."

"Give yourself a few minutes to think about it. Before we talked about words that came into your head when you thought about not feeling right. Now try to think about parts of yourself that make you uncomfortable."

"Like what do you mean?"

"Well," Dr. Taffe concentrated for a moment, "for instance, do you feel uncomfortable about the way that you feel? Or the way that you think?

Or the way that you look?"

"I guess all of those things."

"Okay. So let's take, for instance, the way that you look. What about the way that you look makes you feel uncomfortable?"

Alec looked down at her hands. "It's embarrassing."

"I know. It's okay to talk here. It is a safe place. No one but you and me will know."

Alec took a deep breath. "I really don't like my breasts."

"Okay. Anything else?"

"I feel pudgy. I wish that I was stronger. More muscular."

There was a long silence.

"Alec, I want to ask you a very personal question." Dr. Taffe paused. "Do you feel comfortable having sex?"

"Sort of, I mean, I feel more comfortable with certain things."

"Can you tell me what things you are comfortable with?"

"Well, I'm comfortable making love to my girlfriend. I like that a lot. But I don't so much like her doing things to me. But, ya know, I just figured that I was a stone butch. Ya know, and being stone is supposed to be the purest thing you can be."

"I'm familiar with butch-femme dynamics. I have many stone butch clients," Dr. Taffe reassured Alec. "Let me just clarify, though. Do you feel happy and comfortable being stone, or is that part of what makes you feel uncomfortable?"

"I guess that I kind of wish that I liked having stuff done to me. But it just doesn't feel right."

In truth, Alec had never really felt completely comfortable with sex. Before she had met Smitty, she didn't really have a word to describe her feelings. Now she did: stone butch. A stone butch would make love to her femme, but wouldn't allow herself to be touched. Alec was excited by making love to a woman, but she felt awkward and uncomfortable when the woman would try to reciprocate. She had never really had an orgasm either. She would get excited, but it never seemed to build to a climax the way it seemed to with the women that she had sex with. One of her personal ad ladies had told her once that she should masturbate more to learn how to relax and have orgasms. But Alec didn't feel comfortable touching herself either.

With Jessie, Alec's stone status was something of a point of contention. Jessie seemed to want to make love to Alec, but Alec refused. Jessie didn't push the matter, but Alec worried that Jessie might secretly be hoping that Alec would eventually consent.

Dr. Taffe was quiet for several moments. She seemed to be thinking very hard, almost as if she was arguing with herself in her head.

Finally, she said, "Alec, have you ever wished that you were a man?"

Alec froze. Her mind raced.

"Alec, are you okay?" Dr. Taffe asked, noticing that all of the blood seemed to have drained from Alec's face.

Alec was quiet for several moments and then offered weakly, "Yeah, I'm okay."

"Can you answer my question?"

Alec sat a few moments longer. She looked down at her boots. Dr. Taffe waited patiently.

"I've thought about it," Alec said in a very small voice.

"Thought about what?"

"Thought about what it would be like to be a man. Um…thought about what it would be like to be a man making love to a woman."

"How do you feel saying that?"

"Scared."

"Scared of what?"

"I don't know, that you'll think that I'm weird. That I AM weird."

"Alec," Dr. Taffe said in a reassuring voice, "the concept of 'normal' is a fiction. There's really nothing about feelings that can be weird. We are all just unique. As long as you don't hurt yourself or someone else because of your feelings, then it's pretty much okay to feel anything."

"You're just saying that because I'm paying you." Alec laughed.

"Well, technically, I think that the clinic fund is mostly paying me now, but regardless, I wouldn't lie to you. Really, whatever it is that you feel is okay."

There was silence and the blood began to flow into Alec's face again.

"So, have you always had these thoughts about wanting to be a man, or is it something recent?"

"It feels like I've always had them. As long as I can remember, anyway. I guess that's how I figured out that I was gay. And then, when I met Smitty, she's my mentor at the carpentry program, she started telling me about butch-femme culture and I figured that I was having those thoughts because I was a butch."

"So now that you are in a butch-femme relationship, are you still having those thoughts?"

"Yeah."

"And have you felt any better about yourself, have you felt more 'right' since you began being part of butch-femme culture?"

"I really love Jessie. And Smitty is awesome. She's so funny and she's so great to me. She was so proud when I met Jessie."

"But do you feel any more comfortable with yourself?"

"I'm happier. But I still feel weird. I still feel like I don't fit in."

"Alec, I'm going to give you some homework for next time. I want you to make a list for me. I want you to imagine that you live in a magic world where anything can happen. You can change anything about your life and yourself. You can't change the past. But you can change right now. Make me a list of 5 to 10 things that you would change. It can be anything. How much money you have or who your friends are. You can say that you'd be dating Angelina Jolie [Alec laughs] or that you live in a mansion. You can say that you have super powers or that you're smarter or funnier or that you look differently. Anything. Make that list and bring it back to me next time, in two weeks."

Chapter 10

That next weekend was Chicago Pride. Alec and Jessie joined Smitty and Gail at the Dyke March as part of the butch-femme contingent. Alec kept her therapy revelations to herself.

The march headed down Clark from Foster to Bryn Mawr, right through the heart of Andersonville. They finished up with a modest rally on the Lake Michigan shore. It was a nice day, but hot. The march was fun, but they were all glad to head over to the party behind the Cheetah Gym afterward for some cold beverages.

Several of Smitty and Gail's friends joined them at the party. Alec was a little overwhelmed by the crowd and all of the activity, but she was glad to be finally sitting in the shade in a quiet corner with Jessie. It wasn't long, though, before Smitty and her gang of friends tracked down where Alec and Jessie were sitting.

"Why don't you kids come over and sit with us?" Smitty said.

Jessie nudged Alec and they got up and headed over to the table of middle-aged women. Half of them were dressed in t-shirts, shorts, baseball caps, and sneakers. The other half wore tank tops, elaborate jewelry, and sandals. Alec was sort of amazed by just how much of a dichotomy that the group presented.

Alec was wearing a short sleeved, button-down printed shirt from The Gap, baggy shorts, white socks, and a pair of black Doc Martens. Jessie had on a bikini top that showed off her belly button piercing and the tattoo on the small of her back, a mini skirt, and a pair of Tevas. She had her curly hair pulled back in a ponytail.

Smitty and Gail's crowd were much older than Alec and Jesse, but Alec wasn't in any hurry to hang out with the butches and femmes across the room who were closer to their ages. The whole scene felt a little odd to Alec. She wasn't entirely sure that she understood what it meant yet to be butch or femme beyond the way that someone dressed. Smitty and Gail had been giving Alec plenty of information, but none of the things that they were telling her about how butch-femme relationships worked or felt really resonated with Alec. She felt oddly like an impostor, just like she would if she tried to force herself to fit into heterosexual culture by dating a man and hanging out with businessmen and housewives.

Alec stayed up late after Jessie went to bed that night working on her therapy homework. It was hard. What would she change in her life if she could change anything? She thought about changing her childhood and getting kicked out of her house as a teen. But Dr. Taffe had said that it couldn't be something in the past. Alec felt like her life was finally starting to fall together, so there wasn't much that she wanted. Except to feel normal. Except to feel understood. She wished that she knew what was wrong with her and that she could fix it.

Alec tried to think about why she felt different. She tried to isolate what it was that made her feel uncomfortable in her skin. She felt awkward. She felt like she was always stilt walking; always slightly off balance. She felt like who she was inside of her head and her heart didn't match who she was on the outside.

But who was she in her head and her heart? What aspects of herself did she feel comfortable with? She felt comfortable when she was working hard. She felt comfortable when the guys at work treated her as an equal. She felt comfortable early in the morning drinking coffee on the stoop of her building in an old pair of torn jeans and a white t-shirt and no shoes. If she could change anything, she would make it so that she felt comfortable like that all of the time.

She thought about the question that Dr. Taffe had asked her about if she had ever wished that she was a man. She had been so shocked to hear those words come out of the doctor's mouth. She felt like she was suddenly invisible and that the doctor could read all the secrets from inside of her head.

Alec had wished for so long that she had been born a man that she had forgotten when the desire had even begun. It was so much a part of her running internal commentary, that she didn't even take notice of it anymore. It was a strange and ridiculous thing to think about, and so she had never told anyone about it until at Dr. Taffe's office. But now, when Alec thought about the question again of what she would change if she could change anything, suddenly the answer came to her; she would be a man.

So, if that was the issue, if that was what was making her unhappy, then what good did it do to know that? There was nothing that she could do about it. But, Alec guessed that knowing the reason might give her something to work on fixing in therapy. Or maybe the doctor would give her some miracle pill to make her stop wishing that she was a man.

The next morning Jessie got up early to go to work. Alec was glad it was Sunday and she could sleep in late. She considered going to the main Pride parade that day, but decided that the Dyke March and the subsequent social activity had been enough excitement for her for one weekend. She eventually dragged herself out of bed and shuffled to the bathroom. After relieving herself, she washed her hands and looked into the bathroom mirror.

She turned her face side to side and felt the bones under the skin. She pulled close to the mirror and inspected her face at close range. She noticed a downy cover of peach fuzz hair covering the edges of her jawbones. She had really never noticed how thick this hair was. Alec was blond and fair skinned, so the facial hair was particularly light colored and nearly invisible. She picked at it and followed it as it faded across the rest of her cheek and upper lip. She opened the medicine cabinet and sorted through Jessie's stash of makeup and found a tube of mascara. She closed the cabinet and opened the tube. She had never used the product herself, so she regarded the brush quizzically for a few moments, getting a feeling for how the thick liquid deposited on the coarse brush. Then she turned again to her close examination of her facial hair. Carefully, she took the mascara brush and gently touched it to the area with the thickest fuzz. It took a few moments to get the hang of the process and to assure that she didn't smear big blobs of the mascara onto her face. It wasn't long, though, before she had successfully colored the majority of her facial hair a light brown tone. It was surprisingly realistic looking, other than the fact that the color didn't match her natural tone. It was a light enough coat, though, that it didn't look too strange. Besides, men's beards often tended to be darker than the hair on their heads. She was impressed with just how much facial hair that she had, and how easily it had gone from invisible to concrete. She considered washing it off immediately, but instead she put on a baseball cap and tended to her morning activities at the apartment and left the mascara on her face. Every so often she would stop by the bathroom mirror to take a look. Later, she "shaved" the painted beard, moustache, and sideburns off with foamy soap and the backside of a disposable razor. The exercise felt thrilling and taboo and Alec loved the way that she looked with a beard.

As the days passed Alec continued to work on her carpentry apprenticeship, but she felt distracted. She went to her appointments with Dr. Taffe every two weeks religiously. She stayed up late at night thinking. With each appointment it seemed more and more that what Alec had always kept to herself as a horrible secret, that she wished she had been born a man, was something that Dr. Taffe thought was significant. It was true that, the more that they talked about it, the more relief that Alec felt at knowing what the root of her lifelong discomfort might be. But still, Alec wasn't sure if all the talk would eliminate the problem. If anything, the more that they talked, Alec became more conscious of the yearning to be a man. And the more conscious that she was, the more unfair that it seemed.

Chapter 11

One Saturday night in the early fall, Alec and Jessie went out for dinner at the tacqueria around the corner and then they went to *Club 69* to dance. While she was getting ready to go out, Alec put on her dildo harness and pinned one of her dildos to her body under the harness. She put on a pair of jeans and finished getting dressed. She looked in the mirror and adjusted the bulge in her pants so that it wasn't so noticeable. She nearly got cold feet and took off the harness. But she kept it on and went out with Jessie.

Late in the evening after a few hours of bumping and grinding on the dance floor, making out in dark corners, and a couple of drinks Alec whispered to Jessie, "Come with me to the bathroom."

Alec took Jessie's hand and led her to the back of the bar and into the ladies' room. She pulled Jessie into the handicapped stall with her and closed and latched the door behind them.

Jessie smiled slyly at Alec. This was a first. "What's this all about, sweetie?"

Alec took hold of both of Jessie's hands and pushed them over her head against the side wall of the stall. She leaned against Jessie and began kissing her firmly on the lips. She kissed her neck and her ears. Jessie began to breathe faster. Alec let go of Jessie's hands and let them fall to her sides. Alec put her right hand on the back of Jessie's head and pulled her head to her for another kiss while her left hand gently teased Jessie's right breast.

After several moments, Alec unbuttoned the front of Jessie's blouse and undid the front clasp on her bra. She began to lick and suck Jessie's nipples, alternating between the two while lightly pinching the opposite nipple with one of her hands. With her free hand, Alec began to run her fingers up and down Jessie's thighs.

Outside of the stall, people came and went into and out of the bathroom. Women gossiped and put on their makeup. Toilets flushed. Most people took no notice of the occupied handicapped stall, though a few people giggled and there was one hushed comment from one friend to another of "Is somebody having sex in there?"

Alec continued to suck Jessie's nipples as she unbuttoned her own fly, fumbled with the dildo, and managed to position it in the harness despite the fact that she couldn't see what she was doing. She deftly rebuttoned her jeans above and below the protruding dildo so that her pants wouldn't fall down.

Alec lifted Jessie's skirt and began to tease her mound with her fingers over Jessie's underwear. After a few moments, Jessie reached down and took off her panties right over the top of her heels. Alec reached in her jean pocket and pulled out a sample packet of Maximus lube and ripped the packet open with her teeth. She squeezed the thick liquid out of the packet onto the dildo, began kissing Jessie passionately, and plunged the dildo inside of Jessie's body.

Jessie gasped and braced one of her legs against the toilet and the other against Alec's body. Alec grasped the leg that Jessie was bracing against her and pulled her knee up high while she grabbed Jessie's ass with the other hand. She took Jessie's full weight onto her prosthetic cock and rocked her hips rhythmically.

Jessie began to breathe faster and faster as Alec met her pace both with her own breath and with her hip movements. Alec felt like she was going to explode. And then Jessie came and ejaculated all over the front of Alec's jeans. Jessie leaned forward and grabbed on to Alec and held herself tight to Alec.

Someone two stalls down clapped.

Alec and Jessie looked at each other and broke out in laughter.

Alec took the dildo out of Jessie's body and gently set her girlfriend down on her feet, assuring that she was able to hold herself up. She looked down at herself and saw the huge wet spot on her jeans.

"Wow, babe, that was a big one."

"Yeah it was," Jessie answered. "Where'd you get THAT idea?"

"I don't know, it just seemed like fun."

"Good call."

Jessie slipped her panties into her purse. "What do you say we go home and get you cleaned up?"

Back at their apartment Jessie and Alec took a shower together. Alec felt strong and happy and affectionately shampooed Jessie's hair for her. They finished their shower and got dressed for bed. Crawling into bed together, Alec snuggled up close behind Jessie and put her arms around her.

"I love you baby," Alec whispered into Jessie's ear.

"I love you too sweetie," Jessie answered.

"Are you falling asleep?"

"Not yet, why, what's up?"

"I kinda wanted to talk to you about something," Alec said as her heart began to pound in her head.

"Sure, sweetie, what is it?"

"You know how I've been going to see that therapist?"

"Yeah. How's that going? Are you feeling better?"

"Yeah, actually, I am feeling better. We've been talking a lot about some stuff that is kinda weird, but it's helping."

"Like what kind of stuff?"

Alec swallowed hard. "Like maybe that I might be transgendered."

Jessie paused for a moment. Alec wondered what she was thinking. Jessie had her back to Alec and so Alec couldn't see her facial expression. Eventually Jessie said, "What does that mean exactly?"

"I don't really know yet. Mostly it means that I kinda think of myself more as a man than a woman."

"Well, you ARE the butchest woman that I know," Jessie said.

"Yeah, but I think it's more than just being butch," Alec bravely continued.

Jessie turned around to face Alec. "So, talking about that stuff with your therapist is making you feel better?"

"Yes. Absolutely."

"I can't say that I really understand it, but if it's making you feel better to talk about it, well, then, I'm glad. You've been so confused for so long."

Alec squeezed Jessie tight. "I really do love you so very much."

"Besides," Jessie continued, "if all this means that you're gonna turn into some stud that fucks me in public bathrooms, than I'm all for therapy." Alec smiled broadly to herself and they both happily drifted off to sleep.

Another week passed and Alec went to her regular appointment with Dr. Taffe. Alec happily shared her experience at the bar with Dr. Taffe and told her of Jessie's support.

"How did you feel about yourself during the bathroom encounter?" Dr. Taffe asked.

"Strong. Full of pride. I let myself imagine that I was a man making love to Jessie and pushed down any feelings of guilt that those thoughts might normally cause. It was fantastic. And she loved it so much."

"I'm glad that Jessie is supportive. You will need that kind of support."

Dr. Taffe and Alec smiled at each other.

"Alec, you've been coming to see me for several months now and I feel that you are making remarkable progress in figuring out why you've not felt good about yourself in the past. I feel relatively confident in diagnosing you with Gender Identity Disorder. You've already begun to realize that you feel more comfortable with yourself when you allow yourself to feel masculine. I would like to encourage you to continue to go with those feelings and stop holding back. I'm going to make a note in your records about my diagnosis. What that means, as we move forward through your therapy, is that if you decide at some point that you want to move forward with a gender transition, that I have it on record when your diagnosis occurred."

Alec wasn't sure what the doctor was saying. She didn't want to look stupid, but she also wanted to understand.

"So, what do you mean by gender transition?"

"Well, I want to make sure that you are aware of all of your options, but I don't want you to feel that I am leading you to any sort of decision. That is completely up to you. You can continue your life as you have and we can just continue to talk about your feelings. That would be the minimum that I would suggest that you do in order to continue to feel better about your life. If, as we are proceeding in that manner, you begin to become more and more interested in pursuing a life as a man, you have other options."

Options? What options? "Like what?" Alec asked.

"Well, you already dress in a manner consistent with what is socially expected of men, so you've pretty much already self-selected cross-dressing as a lifestyle. Your name is gender neutral, so, though you may eventually think of changing your name to suit you, your name is not an immediate barrier to feeling masculine, unless you think that it is."

Alec shook her head no. "I've always liked my name."

"Good. You are also entering a work field that is traditionally masculine. So something that you may want to think about, as things progress, is if you would feel better or worse if other people perceived you as a man."

"A lot of people already do. I get called sir a hundred times a day."

"And how do you feel when people call you sir?"

"I feel okay about it."

"Does it make you mad at all?"

"No. I mean it's fine as long as they don't realize their mistake and get embarrassed. That sucks. But I feel fine if they really think that I'm a guy."

Dr. Taffe made some notes.

"So Alec, again I don't want to lead you in any certain direction, but you may want to consider how you would feel about yourself if you were passing as a man more often than not. What do you think about that?"

"That would be fine. It wouldn't be that different from my life already."

"Yes, but the key piece is about how you think about yourself. How you perceive yourself and how you perceive your feelings. And how you feel about how others react to you. I want you to really start to think about those things. I want you to try and be who you feel you really are rather than who you think that others think that you should be. That includes me, by the way. I have no expectation of you other than being as true to yourself as you can be."

Alec was confused. She didn't really know how she could be any more herself than she already was. She had learned long ago not to really care what other people thought of her.

"I don't really know what I should be doing differently that I'm not already doing. And why did you make such a big deal out of marking the diagnosis in your notes?"

"Well, if you find that you are more comfortable as a man than as a woman, there are additional steps that you can take. If you decide that you would like to transition to being a man, you can take hormones that will deepen your voice and cause you to grow facial hair and that will shift the fat deposits on your body from a woman's pattern to a man's pattern."

"Shit, that would be cool."

"Well, it is a big decision. We'll need to continue to work together for at least another six months before we can consider putting you on hormones, and that's why the diagnosis is important."

Alec nodded in understanding.

"On down the line, if you find it is something that you want to pursue, there is a range of surgical options from liposuctioning breast tissue to mastectomy to hysterectomy to genital reconstruction."

The volume of new information flooded over Alec like a tsunami wave. Alec measured the words and replayed them in her mind to be sure that she hadn't imagined them. She felt confused, excited, and scared. She had to be sure of what she was hearing.

"What do you mean by genital reconstruction?"

"Well, there are a number of different procedures that have varying levels of function, but basically it means that a surgeon could construct a penis and prosthetic testicles for you."

"Would it work like a real one?" Alec asked with surprise.

"As I said, there are various types of surgery and there are varying degrees of function. The main two types of surgery are metoidioplasty, which is where they construct a penis from your existing clitoris, which will get larger if you are taking hormones, and phalloplasty, which is where they remove tissue from one part of your body and fashion it into a penis that they attach. Metoidioplasty creates a small penis, but it functions more naturally.

Phalloplasty creates a larger penis, but there is the need for mechanical assistance in order to achieve an erection. Some patients find that they are able to penetrate with the penis created from their clitoris and some are not. Regardless, those folks might feel that the smaller penis feels more natural and responsive. Some people want a larger penis that they can penetrate with easily, or they just like the look of it, and in that case, the phalloplasty makes more sense. It depends on what sorts of issues are important to you. Most importantly of all is to get a very good surgeon who is experienced in the procedure. I want to emphasize, though, that not all female to male transsexuals get ANY kind of surgery, up top or down below. So I don't want you to feel any pressure to move in that direction. It is an expensive, painful process. And the results are not guaranteed to be satisfactory. It is not something to take lightly."

Alec felt excited and hopeful, but overwhelmed.

"I'm going to give you some web sites to visit and the contact for a local FTM support group," Dr. Taffe said.

"What's FTM?" Alec asked.

"It stands for female to male transsexual. The group in town is very good. They'll provide you good support. This is a very difficult thing to go through, and you will need all of the support that you can get. But, if you find that being male is a better, more comfortable expression of who you feel that you are, the transition pains will be well worth it when you come out on the other side. In the meantime I want to continue to see you every two weeks."

Chapter 12

Having dropped out of school so young, Alec had only been exposed to computers on a very limited basis. It had never occurred to her to spend any time on the internet, but Dr. Taffe encouraged her to take a look.

After a little tutoring from Jessie, Alec used Jessie's computer to gather as much information as she could about all the things that Dr. Taffe had mentioned about FTMs. She was surprised at just how much information was available. *There's something for everybody on the internet.* She got tips about how to pass as male and advice about everything from breast binding to hormones to surgery. For a full week she spent every free minute of her time on the computer doing research. She became a regular internet junkie.

One evening, while surfing the net, she found an FTM web blog written by a guy that was Alec's same age and who seemed like a pretty normal person. She read every last inch of the guy's extensive web site. She spent a full three hours on this one site.

The therapy, the research, it had all gotten to be a bit like homework and Alec had sort of emotionally detached herself from the information. She had concerned herself less with the implications for her life and more with the mechanical process of discovery. Suddenly, looking at the web page of this ordinary guy, it hit her like a ton of bricks. *I'm a man. And I can change my body to become a man's body.*

Suddenly, everything that had been repressed or theoretical…the thoughts of wanting to be a man from a young age, always feeling wrong, Dr. Taffe's help, the internet research…it all came crashing down as very concrete and real to Alec. Suddenly she was scared. Not because she wasn't sure if she wanted the change to happen, but because she was sure that she did. Alec now knew that she…no, *he*…had to move towards making his body match his heart and mind.

Alec began making an effort to pass as a man. The changes were subtle, but purposeful. One concrete step Alec took was to bind his breasts every day. At first, Alec tried doing this with an Ace bandage that he had around the house, but it was time consuming and the edges of the bandage cut into his skin. The next step was to purchase a surgical abdominal binder from the drug store. The binder was basically a foot wide piece of heavy duty elastic with Velcro on the ends. It worked pretty well for flattening his chest and was quicker to use than the Ace bandage, but Alec found that it tended to slide down during the day and made it very hard to breath. Finally, he broke down and bought a compression vest off of the internet. Made as a type of girdle for overweight men, the compression vest fit like a sleeveless undershirt, so it didn't slip.

Regardless of the method, though, binding was uncomfortable. Alec had a wide rib cage, and for the first several weeks that he bound his breasts he felt like his ribs were being compressed right along with his breasts. And in fact, they were, because he developed painful bruises all around his midsection. Binders were also thick and hot, and he found that he tended to wear thicker shirts so that the binder wouldn't show through the fabric, making the combination even hotter. On the job site in particular, binding caused a great deal of discomfort. But Alec found that, once he started binding, he felt REALLY awkward when he would take the binder off. He didn't like having breasts, and the more that he bound them, the more that he longed to have them removed entirely. He daydreamed about the day when he wouldn't have to bind anymore and he could walk around on the worksite with his shirt off on a hot day also.

Alec began using men's public restrooms, though the practice made him nervous and he mostly tried to make sure that he used the facilities before he left home. He would always go into the lone toilet stall in the men's room, sit down and fake a grunt to pretend that he was taking a dump, which gave him an excuse for not using the urinal. There were various devices that Alec could purchase or make that would allow him to urinate standing up, but he wasn't quite sure how to use them discreetly in public and he didn't know how to store the devices once he was finished with them. He found that using the stall was a reasonable alternative until he could work out a surgical solution to allow him to pee standing up. Sometimes at home he would practice peeing standing up though, just because it made him feel more masculine.

The transition period was harder than just fear of disclosure in the men's washroom, though. Alec's worst enemy was himself. Though he was obsessed with his transition, he would, on a regular basis, forget that he was a man. He had to remind himself every minute not to make embarrassing mistakes. For instance, when he would still occasionally be referred to as "miss," he would invariably respond without a hint of irritation, forever confusing store clerks. After years and years of mistakenly being called "sir" and learning to live with it, now he felt he needed to learn to be visibly offended by the term "miss" or risk not being truly accepted as a man. He had complicated new social rules to learn and learn fast.

And then there were social rules to be learned for an entire new breed of human beings, too: FTMs. Alec had, at least, been around men all of his life and had some concept of what their world was like. FTMs were another story. Until recently, Alec had not been aware of the world of genderqueers and transmen, even though he had been unwittingly living in that world his entire life. Alec was simultaneously thrilled at the idea of meeting people that were like him and terrified that, once again, he wouldn't fit in. It took Alec a long time to build up the courage to attend an FTM support group meeting.

The group held meetings twice a month. The first meeting of the month was a standard support group meeting with a facilitator at the LGBT (Lesbian, Gay, Bisexual, and Transgender) Community Center. The second meeting of the month was a social outing. Alec hated the idea of going to a traditional support group meeting, which he associated with people who couldn't deal with their own problems. It had been hard enough for him to force himself to attend therapy. But he knew that he wasn't ready for the social outing, and Dr. Taffe was adamant that she thought Alec should reach out to the group.

Not being much of a joiner, Alec had never been to the LGBT Community Center before. It was housed in a modest office on Halsted Street. When Alec arrived there was a skinny gay boy staffing a reception desk near the front door. He had his head shaved close to his skull and was wearing a Tommy Hilfiger t-shirt and what appeared to be tight women's jeans. His face was buried in an issue of *The Advocate*.

"Hi!" the gay guy said in a sing-song voice when he noticed Alec at the desk.

"Hi," Alec replied, tight lipped. "Uh, I'm here for the support group meeting."

"AA or FTM?" the gay guy replied.

Alec winced. He didn't really want to have to be having this conversation out loud. It reminded him of when you go to the doctor's office and the receptionist asks you why you're there in front of all of the people standing in line. "FTM."

"Okay, just go down the hall to the room on the right. If the door is already closed, just knock and let yourself in." The gay boy seemed pleased with himself to be able to help Alec.

Alec headed down the hall to the support group meeting. In the room there were about half a dozen people sitting on couches. The couches were old and seemed to have seen better days. Three of the group, a thin black woman, a heavy set lesbian, and a person who looked to be a teenaged boy with lots of piercing and tattoos, were actively engaged in a conversation.

"I told her that I ain't coming back for that shit," the black woman said.

"Well, didn't she say she was fine with working with FTMs when you had your consultation?," the lesbian asked.

"Yeah, but that stupid bitch don't know what she's doing."

The teenaged boy looked quiet and pensive and let the other two carry the conversation for awhile. Finally, he added, "Jackson, after the meeting let me download a summary of the Harry Benjamin Standards from the internet that you can bring to her. I wouldn't give up on her yet, but if you still aren't comfortable with her after a couple of more sessions, then we'll help you find a new therapist." He gave an earnest look of concern mixed with hope to the black lady and then turned his gaze to Alec. He smiled. "Welcome."

"Hi," Alec replied.

"Are you here for the group?"

"Yeah."

"Great. I'm Kael. I'm sorry that we're getting started a little late, I was waiting to see if more people would show up."

Alec realized suddenly that the teenaged boy wasn't a teenaged boy at all, but was the support group leader. Looking at him more closely, Alec realized that the person was probably actually slightly older than Alec and was probably an FTM. Alec also realized that the two people that he had pegged as a black woman and a lesbian were probably also FTMs, or at least genderqueers. *Jesus, how can I expect to be seen as a man if I can't even give others that courtesy?*

Alec was quiet during the meeting. For that matter, so were most of the others with the exception of Jackson, who continued to grumble about his new therapist. Alec got the feeling that Jackson had been through a number of therapists.

The discussion topic of the meeting was coming out to family. Not having a blood relation family to come out to, Alec listened quietly to the others recount whether or not they had told their families about their gender identity. It seemed like Kael had to work fairly hard to get anyone is the group besides Jackson to talk. And Jackson was hopelessly off topic.

Alec left the meeting with a sense that it hadn't been all that helpful. It was interesting to see other people who were dealing with figuring out that they were men, but none of them seemed to have any answers to the concerns that plagued Alec about how to transition.

It took Alec a while to broach the topic of the new changes with Jessie. Jessie had been supportive so far, but now things were getting serious, and Alec wasn't sure how Jessie would feel about things. A few weeks after he began binding he sat down with Jessie one evening.

"Sweetie, I need to talk to you about some stuff," Alec said.

Jessie joined Alec on the couch. "Is everything okay?"

"Yeah, totally. I just need to talk to you about some transgender stuff."

Jessie took a deep breath and didn't say anything. Alec noticed that Jessie had her hands balled up in little fists in her lap, so he reached out and took her hands.

"Jessie, I'm starting to get more serious about my transition. I don't know if you've noticed, but I've started binding my breasts everyday when I go out of the house."

"You have?"

"Yeah, I've been taking the binding off as soon as I come home. I guess I was afraid it might freak you out." Alec was afraid to look Jessie in the eye after the admission.

Jessie took another deep breath. "I don't like that you didn't feel like you could talk to me about it."

"I know, I'm sorry."

They sat in silence for a while and Alec fidgeted in his seat.

"There's something else. I was wondering if you could start using male pronouns and, uh, try to treat me like I'm a man." Alec looked away from Jessie after saying this.

Jessie got up from the couch and walked over to the window and looked outside. She spoke to the glass instead of directly to Alec. "This is quite a lot to swallow all of the sudden. I want to be supportive, but I feel like you've been leaving me out of the process a little bit. You haven't really talked to me much about this stuff since you first told me about it."

"I know. I just haven't known what to say."

"I love you and I want you to be happy. I'll try my best to respect you in the ways that you've asked, but it's kind of hard to make a sudden switch in perspective like that."

"Tell me about it."

"I know that it's hard on you too. I want you to be comfortable and feel like you can talk to me, but I can't help but worry what effect all of this change will have on our relationship."

"I know. I hope that it won't change anything."

"That's just it. It changes a lot. It changes everything. I just have to play a little catch up. I just hope that you won't shut me out. I don't like getting bombs dropped in my lap. Can you try to keep me better informed on where you're at?"

"I'll try. I'm sorry."

Jessie reached out and gave Alec a hug. "Don't you hide from me, Mister," Jessie said. Alec smiled and hugged her again tightly.

Chapter 13

Alec had started trying to pass pretty much everywhere except in Friday's classes. He passed relatively easily with strangers. To those that knew him before he had started his transition, though, he just seemed more butch than usual. He didn't come out at school because he felt it was just too hard to explain to his classmates, a room full of people that he barely knew, that he was no longer a woman. That was an excuse, though. The real reason that he hadn't made a point of "coming out" in class was because he didn't know what to tell Smitty.

As hard as it was to broach the transition topic with Jessie, Alec knew it would be even harder with Smitty. At least Jessie knew that Alec had transgender issues, but Alec had never told Smitty anything about it. Alec was afraid to disappoint Smitty, and so he put off telling her as long as he could.

One Friday afternoon in late spring after class got out Smitty asked Alec to come along on a shopping spree on Michigan Avenue. Gail and Smitty were going to a wedding later in the month and Gail had gently prodded Smitty that it might be time for a more modern suit. So Alec was enlisted to help Smitty with the wardrobe update.

Alec wasn't used to spending time on Michigan Avenue, and was unfamiliar with the stores. A significant amount of time passed on their field trip before they were even able to locate a decent men's wear store, and even longer before they were able to find one that could accommodate Smitty's significant girth. Smitty didn't enjoy shopping, and usually left these things up to Gail, but Gail thought it would be a good bonding experience for Alec and Smitty to pick out the suit together, and so she declined tagging along.

"You seem to be in better spirits lately," Smitty said, while sorting through sports coats on the clearance rack at *H and M.*

"Yeah, things seem to be looking up. It's kind of a crazy time, but I'm feeling better about life in general."

"See, I told you that once you and Jessie got into the groove that everything would work out just fine," Smitty offered.

"Jessie's great and I do like living with her, but there's a lot of other stuff that I've been working out too."

"Like what?"

Alec thought for a moment, trying to decide how much to say.

"Well, I've been seeing a therapist."

Sensing Alec's embarrassment at the disclosure, Smitty said, "Geez, kid, what self-respecting lesbo hasn't seen a therapist from time to time. That's no biggie, especially considering how hard you had it as a kid and when you first moved to the city. Good for you, it's about time you took care of yourself."

Alec could have let it go there, but he wanted Smitty to be part of his new life. And he knew that, if becoming a man was really what he wanted, that he needed to start living that truth. He couldn't continue to hide it from people who were as important to him as Smitty. Still, in all of the time that he had been putting off telling Smitty, he hadn't come up with a good way to break the news.

"It's a little more complicated than that, a little bit weirder than that," Alec said as he set a tie that he had been fondling back down on the shelf. He felt his hands shaking and it was all that he could do to keep his voice from cracking.

"Whadda ya mean? How bad can it be? Past life regressions? Nurturing your inner child? Energy work? Nothing those earth-mother shrinks do surprises me anymore."

This was it. Alec didn't know what to do other than just say it. Alec took a deep breath. "I've been seeing a therapist because I have gender identity issues. I've figured out that I'm transsexual and that I want to transition to being a man."

It was a lot of words all at one time. More words than Alec typically offered in one string. Smitty was taken aback, both by the volume and the content. She was quiet for a few moments and then said, "Is that what this quack told you, that you're a man just because you like to wear men's clothes? Hasn't she ever heard the term 'butch'?"

Alec was afraid that Smitty might react this way. "Actually, she's a pretty well respected therapist in the gay community. She knows all about butch-femme stuff, probably more than I do."

Smitty began to rifle through the sport coats more aggressively. After a few moments she said, "This stuff is all crap, let's get out of here."

Smitty turned and left the store quickly, not really waiting for Alec to follow. Alec had to jog a little bit to catch up to Smitty, who was halfway down the block already. They reached the end of the block and Smitty stepped out into the crosswalk against the light. An angry motorist slammed on the brakes and laid on their horn. Alec tried to reach for Smitty's arm to stop her from walking in front of the car, but he couldn't reach, and Smitty continued through the intersection, mostly oblivious to the car. Alec followed, motioning apologetically to the driver.

"Hey, slow down. You're gonna get yourself killed," Alec said.

Smitty turned around quickly. "What are you doing? You're not a man. You're a lesbian. You're a butch. Why are you teaching yourself this lie?"

Alec tried to stay calm. "I've thought about this for a long time now. It's the only thing that's ever made sense in my whole life."

"That's crap. This doesn't make any sense at all. What about Jessie? Don't you love her? If she wanted to be with a man, she'd be straight. What are you doing to her? What are you doing to yourself?"

"Jessie loves me. She understands. She's okay with it."

Smitty looked at Alec in disgust and disbelief. "I gotta go," she said and turned and walked off down the street shaking her head from side to side. Alec thought about following her and trying to explain himself more, but he was too heartbroken and ashamed.

Alec made his way back to Andersonville dejectedly. Jessie was home from work and making herself dinner.

"Hey babe, I thought you were gonna hang out with Smitty all evening. Did you guys find a suit?" Jessie asked.

"No. I told her about my transition plans and she freaked out and left."

Jessie sighed heavily. "I'm sorry, babe, that sucks." She wiped her hands on a dish towel and crossed the room to give Alec a hug.

"She didn't even want to talk about it. She didn't even give me a chance to explain. She just said it was crap and took off."

"Honey, it's really hard for Smitty. Her entire life is based on her butch-femme identity. Her career, her wife. She probably feels like you're rejecting who she is for something that she doesn't understand. She probably feels threatened."

"You think?"

"Yeah. It's hard for the old-school folks. They don't understand all of us wacky pierced kids and our modern ways. They're afraid that all the butches will transition and all the femmes will turn into polyamorous bisexuals. They don't understand all of the options that are available to us these days. They're afraid that everything that they know is going to die and then they'll just be these lonely dinosaurs."

Alec nodded quietly.

"And maybe Smitty's afraid that, if she had had the option when she was young, maybe she would have transitioned. Maybe it freaks her out to think maybe her whole life could have been different. Maybe she's jealous. Or maybe it just makes her feel like you're rejecting all that she's taught you about butch life. She can't see that this is who you've always been. Plus, now that the apprenticeship program is almost over, maybe she's afraid that she's gonna lose you, and you transitioning is just one more thing to pull you away from her."

"Thanks, sweetie. You're probably right."

"Of course I'm right." Jessie flashed a sassy smile.

"What am I gonna do, though? She's one of my best friends. She's like my mom…my teacher." Alec paused and swallowed hard. "I want her to be proud of me," he said as his voice began to quiver.

"I know it's hard baby, but she's just gonna need time to get used to things. This is all big news to her. Just think of how long it took you to get used to it."

Alec looked at Jessie hopefully. "How are you doing? Are you still okay with all of this stuff?"

Jessie hugged Alec to her again. "I want you to feel good about yourself, honey. Besides, it's kind of sexy." She pulled back and grinned at Alec.

Alec's heart swelled. "You are the best woman in the world," he said.

That night in bed Alec couldn't sleep. He was worried. What if Smitty was right? What if he *wasn't* making the right choice? What if Jessie really *didn't* understand? What if everyone that Alec had ever loved would reject him for transitioning? What if he transitioned and nothing got better? All he could do was try it and see what happened. He had been on his own in life before, and if he had to be on his own again, well, at least it would be familiar territory.

Buoyed by the confidence that he could get by even if he was on his own, Alec thought more critically about Smitty's assessment of the situation. It was true that Alec was happier with Jessie than he had ever been with any woman, and he thought that part of that *was* the butch-femme dynamic that they shared. Alec didn't know how to explain it, how two people who were at opposite ends of a spectrum could balance each other so perfectly. He admired how brave and strong and proud that Jessie was. He loved that she probably could and probably often did pass as straight to most of the world, but that she still had so much pride about being queer. He loved that Jessie let him be chivalrous with her.

Alec wasn't so sure why it mattered if he was a biological female or a transguy, either way he could still be a butch. Either way he thought that he would love the same kinds of people. He was still the same person, he just might have a body that he was more comfortable in.

Alec was sad that Smitty couldn't understand, but he decided that was no reason not to pursue his own happiness. He could define himself, his life, and his love anyway that he wanted. He didn't need anyone's approval or permission.

Chapter 14

The last Friday in May was a bittersweet day for Alec. It was the last day of Smitty's apprenticeship course. The other students had made plans to go out for a big dinner celebration after class at the Chicago Sports Bar and Grill. Alec didn't socialize much with the rest of the class, but he wanted to go to the dinner. He knew that Smitty and Gail would be there, though, and he didn't want to upset them by attending. He was also still mad and hurt by the way that Smitty had been treating him ever since the day he had told her about his transition plans.

The jubilant new carpenters filed out of the building after class and headed down the street towards the restaurant like small children on the first day of summer recess. Alec gathered his things and followed slowly behind.

"Are you coming to dinner, sugar?" Gail asked Alec as he passed by the reception desk.

"I don't know, should I?"

Gail leaned over the desk and lowered her voice so that Smitty, who was in the shop finishing cleaning up, wouldn't hear. "Honey, we miss you so much on Sunday nights. It makes me feel like we've lost our only child. Give her a chance, she'll come to understand eventually."

Alec didn't know whether to feel touched or irritated. "Look, I'm not the one who has a problem with the situation," he said, raising his voice a bit.

"Take it easy, Alec. Smitty has enough pride over the whole thing for both of you. Just think about trying to make things right with her."

Alec wanted to argue. How was he supposed to make things right when Smitty just didn't get it? When Smitty was so hostile to who he really was? He knew that none of this was Gail's fault, though, so he stopped himself from responding.

Instead he said, "I'll come to dinner, how about that?"

"Great. We'll see you there in a bit." Gail smiled and squeezed Alec's shoulder.

Outside it was a nice day. Aside from the difficulties with Smitty, Alec was feeling optimistic about life. In just a few weeks, he would start his testosterone treatments. He couldn't wait.

At dinner Alec chatted with his classmates about their work plans. Alec had secured a position with a firm that was renovating some condos in the loop. It was a nine-month project. Smitty had assured that the entire class had access to resources to keep steady work coming for the foreseeable future.

Gail mingled amongst the students, but Smitty stayed glued to her seat at the far end of the table drinking her beer and talking quietly with whoever came over to her. Alec stayed away from her throughout dinner, but after dinner, when the other students started going home, Alec headed over to Smitty's post.

"Hey," Alec said as he sat down next to Smitty.

Smitty didn't say anything and continued nursing her beer. An uncomfortable period of time passed in silence. Here and there other students came up and said goodbye to Alec and Smitty.

After a while Alec said, "So are you going to talk to me or should I just leave?"

"I don't have anything to say, so you can do whatever you want," Smitty answered.

Gail observed them nervously from the other end of the table where she was looking at some baby pictures that one of the students had produced.

"So, you just hate me now for no good reason?" Alec said.

Smitty looked Alec coldly in the eye and then looked away. "Yeah, that must be it. I must hate you for no good reason," Smitty said with sarcasm dripping in her voice.

"Why can't you just try to understand?" Alec said in an exasperated tone.

"That old bulldagger, Smitty, she's too old and too dumb to understand all this hip modern stuff," Smitty said, referring to herself in the third person and leaning back in her chair while taking a long swig from her beer.

"Whatever. If you can't even try to understand then I guess you really don't care about me anyway." Alec got up from his chair and shoved it forcefully under the table so that the back tipped and the chair nearly toppled. He headed towards the door. Gail got up from her seat and Alec motioned a stop sign with his hand towards her.

"I tried, okay, it's up to her now," Alec said as he passed Gail and headed out the door.

The next day Alec was depressed. He wanted to feel good, but was really bummed out about Smitty. Jessie was working and Alec felt lonely at home. He got on his bike and started riding, not quite sure where he was going. Before he knew it he was out near the junction of Highways 90 and 290, basically the outer reaches of the city. He was tired and hot, so he decided to stop in to the air-conditioned comfort of the Woodfield Mall. He slowly walked the wide aisle of the mall and let the sweat dry on his back. He stopped into The Gap and they were having a big sale.

It had been a long time since he had bought himself anything new. He pawed through the racks of airy men's long sleeved shirts. Ironically, several of them were in pastels, pink even. *Great, right when I decide to become a guy they change the rules on me.* Alec did manage to find a cheap pair of shorts and a really nice blue, green, and purple striped shirt. He left The Gap and headed on to Eddie Bauer. Nothing much there, but he did sample the various flavors of men's colognes. The new musky smells were mixing oddly with his own sweaty outdoor odor, so he went into the Eddie Bauer dressing room and changed into his new outfit from The Gap, using his old clothes to wipe the sweat off of his body. Since he was on the bike he hadn't bound his breasts so that he could breathe better. His tight sports bra was soaking wet. He wished that he could take it off, but it gave him a thin layer of protection. He couldn't bear the thought of his 36 Bs bouncing under his handsome new shirt.

Next he was on to Abercrombie and Fitch. A larger than life black and white poster of a blond guy without a shirt greeted him as he entered the store. The guy had a perfect hairless chest with small hard nipples and six pack abs. Alec stared at the picture for a long time. A skinny woman approached him and asked if she could help him find something. He continued to stare at the picture for a few more moments, painfully aware of the wet bra under his shirt. He turned to the woman and said with a cold, emotionless face, "Do you have men's underwear?"

"Oh. Sure." She led him to the section of the store where the men's underwear was stocked. He picked through the selection and found the smallest packet of sleeveless undershirts and a package of size 30 boxer briefs. *Jesus these are expensive.* It didn't matter. He went into the men's dressing room. He tore open the package of undershirts, took off his nice new shirt and his bra. He closed his eyes and wiped his sweaty breasts with the dirty shirt that he had taken off, and then he put on all three of the tight undershirts. They weren't comfortable, but they were clean and dry and they did the trick as well as the bra had. He changed his bottom underwear too and got redressed in his new clothes.

He took the empty t-shirt package and the underwear packet that now only had one remaining pair of boxer briefs in it and went to the counter. The skinny woman met him. "Did you find everything okay?"

"Yes, thank you," Alec said, and handed her the ripped packages. The woman looked at the packages, then at Alec quizzically.

Alec tried to save them both from as much embarrassment as possible. In a low voice he said, "Look, I'm wearing them. I know it doesn't make any sense, but I swear I didn't steal anything, so could you please just ring me up and let me leave without a problem?"

The clerk looked like she had never been so confused in her life, but she did as Alec asked and rang him through without any questions asked.

He left the store, now sufficiently dry and bound. He caught a glimpse of himself in the reflection of a store's glass window. He stopped and looked at his image. The cologne from Eddie Bauer filled his nostrils. Despite the indignities of the day, he suddenly felt sexy. He closed his eyes and breathed in deeply and let the cologne fill his senses completely.

Chapter 15

In two weeks time Alec found himself back at Dr. Taffe's office for his last appointment before starting hormones. They spoke briefly about the encounter with Smitty and Dr. Taffe recommended that Alec give Smitty time and space to process the situation before trying to make contact again. She also encouraged Alec to try and stay in touch with Gail if possible, since Gail seemed to be more supportive and had some influence with Smitty.

"So how are you feeling about your prescription?" Dr. Taffe asked.

"Great, I can't wait."

Dr. Taffe had sent Alec to a medical doctor to have a complete blood workup and physical to assure that Alec was healthy enough to take hormones. It was vital to assure, in particular, that his liver was healthy. When the test results came back normal, the doctor arranged for a testosterone prescription for Alec.

"We'll continue to see each other once a month to see how you take to the hormones. If anything unusual happens in the meantime, please give me a call and we can set something up sooner. Do you have any other questions?"

Alec shook his head. He had been seeing Dr. Taffe for a full year now, every two weeks at first, and once a month for about the last six months. They had talked about pretty much everything in Alec's life and Dr. Taffe had gone over everything she knew to explain about transsexualism and about the process of transitioning. For over six months Alec had been doing his best to pass exclusively as a man. He kept his hair cut short and bound his breasts every day. His carpentry work had begun to build his upper arm strength, and so the muscles in his biceps were now quite substantial. On a new worksite he always marked "male" on any forms that he had to fill out, and so far, that's how he had been accepted for the most part. There was a bit of confusion sometimes at the start as to why he was coming from an apprenticeship program for women, but most people just glossed over this detail and didn't even ask.

Alec left Dr. Taffe's office and went straight to the pharmacy on Halsted Street. He had prescreened for the gayest pharmacy that he could find in town, so that he wouldn't be harassed. He gave the prescription to the pharmacist and paced the aisles of the pharmacy nervously waiting for his prescription to be filled. In about ten minutes that passed like ten hours, the pharmacist called "Alec Jensen" and Alec went to the window to pick up the goods. The pharmacist, who was used to handing out hormones both male and female to patrons in the neighborhood, didn't bat an eye, and took a long time checking to be sure that Alec understood how to take the injections, and even offered to help him do the first one, but Alec was embarrassed to look stupid, so he just took the bag with the bottles of hormones and the syringes and headed home.

Alec got home and headed directly to the bathroom with his bag from the pharmacy. He put the toilet lid down, sat on it, and nervously read all of the instructions that were included in the bag. He took out a bottle of testosterone and a cellophane wrapped syringe. He carefully unwrapped the syringe, frightened to poke himself even though the syringe had a safety cap. Ironically, he would soon be poking himself all the time and his fear of handling the needle was a bit ridiculous. He pulled down his jeans to his ankles and searched out a good location for the first injection. He grabbed the vial and the syringe and nervously drew the thick, oily liquid up. He tapped the syringe and pushed a bit of the liquid out to get out any trapped air. His hands were shaking. In one quick motion he stabbed himself in the thigh with the needle, feeling the sharp sting. He drew back the plunger a bit to check for blood as the instructions had described. He stared long and hard to verify that there was not any blood. Then he closed his eyes and he depressed the plunger.

Afterwards, he pulled his pants up, put the safety cap back on the syringe, and put it into the special red plastic sharps container that the pharmacist had given him. He paused to try and see if he felt any different. Nothing. The whole process seemed a bit anticlimactic. He wasn't sure what to do with himself. Something profound had just changed in his life, but the world seemed to still be spinning just the same way it had before.

He wondered to himself if Hallmark made a card for going on hormones, or if FTD had a bouquet. "So you've started juicing up? Congratulations!" Or even better, a nice bunch of flowers with a cigar stuck in the arrangement and a blue balloon that said "It's a boy!" He decided that he wouldn't hold his breath waiting for the accolades to arrive. And Jessie was working late, so a celebration dinner would have to wait until tomorrow night.

Not knowing what else to do, Alec sat down on the couch and turned on the TV. Fridays were a bad TV night. He watched the local evening news, half expecting one of the anchors to say, "And in Andersonville tonight, Alec Jensen took his first injection of male hormones. When asked why, he simply said, 'Hey, I'm a guy, I want a beard and a little dick.' And now over to Sally with the weather…"

Most of the changes in Alec from the hormones took some time to surface. One change that occurred relatively quickly, though, was a change in Alec's genitals. His clitoris, which he now preferred to refer to as his penis, seemed to be growing. He had known to expect this change, and he was happy to see that it happened so quickly. Though much, much smaller than the average man's penis, it was still an improvement.

The weeks began to pass and the testosterone injections became more and more routine. By late summer Alec was beginning to notice more differences. He felt like the shape of his body was changing. After six months, his voice began to crack like a teenaged boy and he began to see hairs appear on his chin. The morning that he noticed the first one he whooped with joy and woke up Jessie.

He wanted so badly to celebrate every new change with Jessie, but Alec began to feel like Jessie didn't want to talk about things related to his transition. She never mentioned the changes to Alec and he felt awkward bringing it up.

Chapter 16

One afternoon a few months after Alec started taking hormones, Alec and Jessie both had off of work and they decided to catch a movie at the independent cinema. They met Sam and Christie, Jessie's friends from the night that she met Alec, at the theatre to see *Joy of Life*, a film by Jenni Olson about a lesbian searching for love set against an examination of suicides from the Golden Gate Bridge. After the movie they went out for coffee.

"So are you guys going to any of the Gay Games stuff next week?" Sam asked. "It's so cool that the Games are coming to Chicago."

"I have to work most of the time, plus it's kind of expensive, isn't it?" Jessie said.

"I don't know, I didn't look into the ticket prices. You know Janice is gonna play on the softball team," Sam continued.

"No shit? That's so cool. I suck at sports," Jessie said.

Christie joined in, "If shopping was a sport, you and me would kick some serious ass." At this admission, Christie and Jessie slapped each other a high five.

"What about you, Alec? Did you think about trying out for the games for something?" Sam asked.

Alec, who had been listening apathetically to the conversation, said, "Why would I?"

"Well, it's not like the Gay Games comes to Chicago every year. And, I mean, they have shit like table tennis, I think. Pretty much anybody could find something to try. Unless they're too busy shopping," Sam said as she shot a loving look towards Christie and Jessie.

"Well, yeah," Alec said, "the only problem is that I'm not gay."

The room fell silent. Jessie looked down at her coffee and stirred it with a twisted plastic stick that she had been chewing on.

"What?" Sam said.

"I'm not gay. I'm straight. Remember?" Alec said impatiently.

"Oh, right, well whatever," Sam answered, sensing that she had offended Alec, but not really feeling like what Alec was saying was terribly material to the conversation at hand.

"Whatever?" Alec parroted back. "Nice. Thanks." Alec got up from the table and stormed out the door of the café.

"Are you gonna go after her?" Sam asked Jessie.

"Him, Sam, him. Jesus, get with the program," Jessie answered. "No, I'll let him blow off some steam first. If I try to talk to him right away he'll just bite my head off."

"So how are things going with all that, anyway?" Christie asked in a hushed tone that hinted at both fascination and a bit of embarrassment. The embarrassment seemed to be sympathetic to Jessie, though.

"It's fine. It's hard. It doesn't help when people say stupid shit." Jessie glared at Sam.

"What? What am I supposed to say? It's not like she's a real guy or anything. She's just like an uber-butch. Shit, she's not even really that butch as far as that goes. And what's all this, 'I'm not gay' crap. She's got girl parts, you've got girl parts…what do you call that if it's not gay?"

"Look, Sam, I know it's hard to understand, but you're not doing me any favors by being so damn Neanderthal about it. Can't you cut me a little political correctness?"

Sam frowned and settled back in her chair. "She should just learn to be happy with who she is. She's got a great job and a great girl and the whole damn thing doesn't make any fucking sense to me at all."

Christie intervened, "Really, Jess, though, are you okay with all of this stuff?"

Jessie didn't want to give Sam the satisfaction, but the truth was that she longed to talk to someone about how she felt about Alec's transition. Before she knew it she was saying more than she meant to say.

"I thought I could handle it. I mean, I'm really attracted to butches and I thought that Alec becoming a transman was just the next step on that scale. It seemed kind of sexy and exotic at first. I guess that I also thought that maybe if Alec felt more comfortable with his body that he wouldn't be stone anymore. And maybe that will still happen, but now I wonder if *I'll* feel comfortable with his body after the transition."

It had actually taken awhile for Jessie to notice the changes in Alec after he had started T. The voice cracking made her giggle to herself, though she tried not to embarrass Alec by letting it show. Eventually, she also noticed that Alec's upper arms seemed to be getting even stronger than before. He was moodier than before, too, and more self-absorbed. He seemed even quieter and more withdrawn than he had been before.

Jessie tried not to take the changes personally, but it was hard. She tried to be supportive, but she began to grow weary of the excuse that the hormones were to blame, or that the transition was just really stressful. When Alec's beard began to come in, she thought that she would think it was sexy. But oddly, the little hairs just seemed to represent all of the changes that were happening, and suddenly she wasn't entirely sure if she liked them. The hairs continued to come in, though, week after week, and the other changes continued to come right along with them.

Jessie's life had followed a different path than Alec's. Jessie grew up in the northwest suburbs of Chicago. Her family was middle class. Her father was a salesman for a firm that distributed hydraulic machinery parts worldwide and her mother was a nurse in a doctor's office.

Jessie had one sister, Erin, who was two years older than her. Jessie's father traveled quite a bit, so that no one in the family saw much of him. When Jessie was 12, her parents separated and eventually got a divorce. Jessie's father moved out and Jessie and Erin lived in the house with their mom. Aside from normal sibling rivalry, Jessie and Erin got along well. In fact, Erin was the first person that Jessie ever came out to at age 15. Erin got married relatively young and grew up to be a social worker. She and her husband and their two kids lived on the far southeast side of Chicago, almost to Gary, Indiana, and Erin worked with inner city kids in Gary.

Jessie's parents were both relatively accepting of Jessie's sexuality too, though Jessie secretly thought that they both probably thought that it was a phase that she would grow out of.

Jessie had gone to college at the University of Wisconsin at Madison and had gotten a women's studies degree like most of the other lesbians in the world. And, along with them, she found that there weren't any jobs for people with women's studies degrees. For that matter, there weren't many jobs in Madison either, as PhDs battled for minimum wage employment to pay their sky-high mortgages in one of America's "best cities to live in." Madison was indeed a nice place to live, and Jessie had access to a more than accepting lesbian environment there, but Chicago was home.

Jessie returned to Chicago and took the job at Trader Joe's natural food store north of the loop right out of college. It seemed like the lesser of several evils. A job where she could pretend that she was being socially responsible, even though she knew that the store was just one more corporation in the world's constellation of profit-driven motives. The job paid the bills though, it wasn't hard, and she liked her coworkers. She would put off figuring out what she wanted to be when she grew up until another day.

Jessie had been attracted to women as long as she could remember. She liked everything about women. Boys wanted to date her in high school, but she never felt comfortable going out with them. When she got to Madison, it didn't take long for her to find The 10% Society, the campus gay group, and to start dating a long line of women. Most of the dykes in Madison seemed like flannel-shirted, corn-fed women to Jessie, but somehow she forged a strong femme identity there anyway. Jessie liked butches, which was good because there was a serious lack of femmes on campus. The stereotypical butch-femme dynamic ended for Jessie at the bedroom door, though. She was used to being an equal partner in sex.

In truth, Jessie had never really been happy with her sex life with Alec. Alec was a very tender and competent lover, but Jessie longed to return the favor. In the beginning, Jessie had at least been able to look at Alec naked. She thought for sure that the longer that they dated, the more that Alec would relax and let her start being the active sex partner sometimes. As Alec became more convinced of his transgender status though, he had become more protective of his body and he didn't seem to like Jessie even looking at him naked, much less touching him. Jessie had hoped that the changes in Alec would make him more likely to be receptive to her physical contact, but she wasn't seeing improvement.

The combination of Alec being stone and being transgendered sort of left Jessie at a loss as to what her role was. The two things that helped identify her identity as a lesbian, dating a woman and making love to a woman, both seemed to be slipping away from her. She loved Alec a great deal, but she had started to wonder if love was enough.

Chapter 17

A lec showed up at the Trader Joe's around 8:45 to meet up with Jessie one night. It was rare that Jessie got to leave right when the store closed at 9, but tonight she drew the straw to go home early. Alec milled about in the aisles, looking at the exotic foods and the over-priced beauty care items. *How could people afford this shit?*

Alec was a meat and potatoes kind of guy, mostly because he didn't know anything else. His chronic status hovering just above poverty level, or occasionally dipping below it, meant that he was happy to get a meal period, never mind making sure that it met government nutritional standards. Vegetables were basically a foreign substance to Alec, and when he would visit Jessie at work he was forever fascinated by the array of products that were completely bizarre to him.

Because of where Jessie worked, Alec had been reading on the internet about herbal supplements that he could use to improve the transition process, so he settled into the vitamin aisle with the dog-eared store copy of *Prescription for Nutritional Healing* that he had found on the shelf and began reading and looking at bottles. Most of the bottles he glanced at the price on first, and quickly replaced the bottles on the shelf in discouraged horror.

Hmmm...what might be the likely code words? Hair Loss? Impotence? Glandular Therapy? Growth Hormone Therapy? Why couldn't they just have a section on "male deficiency"?

Feeling self-conscious and a little paranoid, when Alec sensed someone walking down the aisle towards him he quickly closed the book and put the bottle of raw orchic glandular, an extract used to promote male sexual function, back on the shelf. The handsome, well-dressed stranger walked past Alec and picked up a container of Spiru-tein protein powder and glanced back in Alec's direction and gave him a quick once-over.

"You don't want to take that shit, it might fuck with your T," the stranger offered quietly as he coolly and casually left the vitamin aisle.

Alec's head swirled, not believing his ears. *How did that guy know?* His brain slowly put the puzzle pieces together. *Could that guy be a transman? Whoa. He looked really good.*

Alec nervously set out after the stranger. He caught a glimpse of him grabbing some items from the cooler and heading to the cash register. The stranger was about 5 foot 10 inches with dark curly hair cropped close to his head. He wore small oval glasses with dark frames and was dressed in a well-tailored black suit and tie. He looked to be very fit. And he was extremely handsome.

As luck would have it, the stranger picked Jessie's station. As he waited in line, Alec lurked behind a display of cases of soy milk. His heart was pounding and he didn't know what to do. He wanted to approach the stranger, but didn't know how. He let him pass through Jessie's register, noting that he paid with a credit card, and then watched him leave the store.

As soon as Jessie's line was empty and she went back to fronting candy near the checkout area, Alec rushed over to her.

"Hey, did you see that transguy?" Alec asked.

"What transguy?"

"He was like, third from the end of the line. He bought three or four things. Um, he bought Spiru-tein."

"Oh, the GQ guy in black? Yeah, I remember him. That was a chick?" Jessie said incongruously.

"No," Alec said exasperatedly, "he's a guy...a transman...a FTM."

"Oh, yeah, right. Sorry. I just meant, well, I never would have guessed. Now that you mention it, though, he didn't seem like a normal guy. He was sort of too nice to me. He made eye contact. Anyway, I think I've seen him before...he comes in and gets just a few things occasionally."

"He's the first transman I've seen just out in real life, ya know?" Alec confided.

"Wow, that's cool."

"Hey, is there any way you can get his name from the credit card?"

"Oh yeah, sure, that's easy." Jessie went over to the register and pulled out the white slip from the transaction. "Tucker Buchanan," she read out loud, "that's a great butch name."

"*Trans* name," Alec corrected. He added a moment later, "I mean, a *man's* name."

Jessie finished up her duties, hung up her apron, grabbed her bag, and she and Alec left the store. "Are leftovers okay, sweetie?" Jessie asked. "I could heat up the leftover casserole from last night. And I got some free day-old cookies from work for dessert."

Alec was deep in his own head. "Huh?"

"Dinner? Can I just reheat leftovers?"

"Oh, yeah, baby, that'd be great. Thanks."

The two of them got on the L and headed home.

Alec lay awake all night wondering about the captivating stranger he had seen at the store that night. One of Alec's misgivings about transition was that he had very few good role models. The transmen that Alec knew of through the FTM social group didn't seem like "real" men to him. Some of them could pass as men, but the majority of them were basically genderqueer. They weren't men and they weren't women. Their facial hair came in patchy and scraggly. They were short. They seemed unsure of their masculinity.

But this stranger, Tucker, was something entirely different. He looked like a real man. He acted like a real man. He was handsome and self-assured. Alec wanted to talk to Tucker so badly. He had a thousand questions for him. Alec wanted to know how to become the type of man that Tucker was.

Alec got up out of bed and quietly walked to the living room and booted up Jessie's computer. He googled Tucker Buchanan. It was handy that he had such a unique name. The search returned one listing, a page for the firm Terrin Power with Tucker listed as a contact for some service that the company provided. It was hard to tell what Terrin Power was, it seemed to be something like an insurance firm, but Alec didn't really understand. Anyway, it didn't matter, at least now Alec knew where Tucker worked. Alec continued his web stalking, going through yellow pages and various free people-finding tools. He didn't manage to come up with anything more, though.

Chapter 18

Tucker parked his Karmann Ghia, grabbed the bag of groceries off of the passenger seat, and headed to the elevator. After stopping at the lobby to pick up his mail, he headed to the 3rd floor, got out of the elevator, and opened the door to his condo. He threw the mail on the coffee table, left the Spiru-tein on the kitchen counter, and put the kefir and the eggs in the refrigerator next to the wilting bunch of beets left over from last week's juice fast. He was glad to be back on solid food, but even more so, he was glad that he could finally have a beer again. He reached far into the back of the fridge and pulled out a bottle of Third Coast micro-brew beer, flipped on the gas fireplace, and flopped down on the couch. He hit the remote and soon was losing himself in a PBS documentary on Typhoid Mary. He wished he could head down to the bar, but it would be dead on a Thursday night. Plus it was too cold to go out again. Tomorrow night would be soon enough.

The transition back and forth between the historical depiction of Typhoid Mary in her own voice and the words of modern historians was distracting. *Just get to the facts, no one knows what the chick would have really said.* Plus the woman playing Mary was kind of ugly. Tucker wondered if there would be any good looking women at the bar tomorrow. Maybe he should go back to Friendly's, the straight bar across town. He used to like it there. The women were really hot. Ever since that one chick freaked out on him last year when he went back to her place he just hadn't felt good about going back there, though. *Stupid bitch, she ruined the whole damn place.* He'd never had any complaints before, why'd she have to be such a stickler for details? She was lucky to have a chance to have sex with a guy as hot as him. It's not like he was some troll. She should have been happy to have sex with a hot guy that wouldn't get her pregnant or some nasty disease. She didn't know what she was missing. It was a while ago, but odds are that she told her friends. Maybe he should try something new. It was just getting stale at Club 69, plus half the time those dykes were just trying to fulfill some weird fantasy. He preferred picking up straight women. Yeah, maybe it was time to break in a new hang out. *What a pain in the ass.*

So, wait, Typhoid Mary spends all this time quarantined against her will, and then runs right out and gets another job at a restaurant. *What the hell was wrong with her? Did she want to stick it to those fuckers so bad that she did it on purpose, or did she just not get it? Geez.*

Tucker picked up the pile of mail and sorted through it. Cable bill...Society of Actuaries newsletter...and a letter from...*oh shit*...from Goshen High School addressed to "Sarah Buchanan." "You are cordially invited to the twenty-year reunion of the class of 1986." *No way.* Why did his mom have to keep giving them his forwarding address? God love the woman, but couldn't she understand that the disgust that the class of 1986 would have for him could only be surpassed by the disgust that he had for the class of 1986? He reached over to the shredder and put the letter and envelope through it.

It wasn't as if he hadn't grown up to be everything that the teachers at Goshen High could have hoped for…good-looking, smart, rich, with a steady job and a great condo. He was a model alumnus. Of course, they probably never knew he was a guy.

They surely knew by now, though, unless there was still someone left in that po-dunk town that his brother Mark hadn't told yet. *That asshole.* Like being daddy's little man and following in his footsteps on the police force wasn't enough. He had to run his mouth off too. Ah well, the joke was on him because he was still stuck in that town.

Tucker grew up in the small Indiana town of Goshen right in the heart of Amish country. His father, a retired Goshen police officer, and his mother, who had stayed home to raise the children, still lived there along with his brother Mark, now also a police officer. Tucker's other brother, John, lived out in the country, and worked at an RV manufacturing plant in nearby Waukarusa. John was eight years older than Tucker and Mark was six years older. John was the strong silent type, Mark the insecure middle child, and Tucker the brain and the baby. John struck out on his own early. Took the job at the RV plant right out of high school, and married and had kids not long after that. Mark played for his father's affections, and took an early interest in joining the police force.

As a child Tucker never saw much of his father, who worked long and odd shifts. He bonded closely with his mother, though, who had extensive time to devote to her youngest child. His mother played on the floor for hours with her only daughter. She was a kind, intelligent woman and Tucker loved her deeply. But as Tucker got older, he began to figure out his gender identity more, and he rebelled against all things feminine, including his mother. He rarely let himself think about it, but every so often, when he got drunk and was feeling sorry for himself, Tucker missed his mother.

Tucker was glad, though, that he had been self-aware enough to figure out his gender identity early in life. He knew of plenty of people who struggled for many years before figuring it out. Tucker had a sense from a young age that he was a guy. He couldn't remember ever having identified as female. As a young girl he was quickly identified by everyone he came across as a tomboy. Once puberty came on, he could tell that people around him were becoming more and more uncomfortable with his lingering masculine behavior and manner. He still felt perfectly comfortable with himself, though. It was the late 1970s and glam rock was just wrapping up its popular run as punk rock came on to the scene. Tucker mused about the images of David Bowie and other men dressed in a feminine way and wearing makeup. He thought it odd that these folks were perfectly acceptable, but that he, as a girl who acted like a boy, was not. It got him to wondering if it might not be possible to pass as a man someday if he moved somewhere that no one knew him. He began to fantasize about making that change.

When Tucker left college at Purdue and moved to Chicago, he was determined to make a clean break and to start his life over. He never told his family about his transition or his gender identity, and once he began hormones, he never again returned to Goshen to visit. Tucker's father told him once that he was an ungrateful child to take the money for college and abandon the family. Tucker's only communications with his family these days were the flowers that he sent his mother every year on her birthday and Mother's Day and the card that he sent her at Christmas.

A few years after Tucker graduated from college, his brother Mark heard from a neighbor who attended Purdue around the same time as Tucker that Tucker was known to dress up as a man and date women. Mark had gotten Tucker's phone number from his mom and called "Sarah" to tell her that people were spreading rumors about her. Mark, always looking for a way to raise himself up by dragging others down, had probably just been hoping to take glee in making "Sarah" feel bad about the rumor. Instead, when he called, Tucker confirmed it and added that he was actually now living as a man named Tucker. Mark was nearly shocked speechless, but regained his composure enough to tell Tucker that he was going to hell. Tucker had responded by telling Mark that he would see him there. Tucker suspected that, true to form, Mark then immediately spread the rumor to the rest of the family and the rest of the town. The evidence of this came on his next birthday card from his mom that was addressed to "Tucker Buchanan" rather than "Sarah Buchanan." As always, his mom had only signed it, "love mom."

Chapter 19

Typhoid Mary was done and a program about Cary Grant started. *Cary Grant...was he a fag? No...that was Rock Hudson. That Grant was a good-looking guy.* Tucker had never really been into old movies, but watching Grant, he thought maybe he should put some of his films on his NetFlix queue. Tucker glanced at the cable bill while he got up to get another beer. He didn't know why he bothered getting cable *and* NetFlix if he was just going to watch PBS all the time, but he guessed it didn't matter.

That funny sense of timing that Cary Grant had, it reminded Tucker a little bit of Doug. He should probably call him sometime to see how things in Boston were going. It had been awhile. Ever since Doug got married it felt a little weird. They hadn't taken a trip together in years.

Tucker went to Purdue not because he wanted to, but because his parents paid for it. To a family in small town Indiana, Havard and Yale had nothing on Notre Dame and Purdue. If Tucker's dad had been able to get into Purdue, that's where he would have gone to school. Growing up in Lafayette,

Indiana he was a devoted Boilermakers fan. When the time came for the decision of where Tucker, then Sarah, should go to college, there was no discussion. It was to be Purdue.

Though not his decision, Tucker was happy to oblige and he entered Purdue in the fall of 1986. Purdue seemed far, far away from Goshen, which was the best place that Tucker could imagine being. Plus, Lafayette was a mere two and a half hour drive from Chicago, a city big enough and metropolitan enough where Tucker was sure that he could begin to pursue his interest in cross-dressing in earnest. When he left high school, Tucker was still interested in passing as a man, but he knew that it would be tough to do in college, so he started a double life, one identity in Lafayette and one in Chicago.

The other advantage to Tucker of Purdue was that it was a heavy science and engineering school. Tucker had a lifelong interest and propensity in mathematics. Solving math problems made him happy. They were like little puzzles that gave him an adrenaline charge when he would complete them. He soon learned that the most lucrative field that he could pursue in mathematics that would also require the least amount of school was actuarial science, an obscure field that few people understood or even knew existed. A field that would allow him to spend his days continuing to work puzzles out in his mind while also allowing him to make enough money to pay for hormones and surgeries.

In many ways, Purdue was two schools. Or perhaps it was one school with an identity crisis. On the one hand, the school that Tucker's dad loved so much was a place that was all about football and fraternities. Tucker had no interest in that place. Luckily for Tucker, the other side of Purdue was about the serious study of science, engineering, and math. And that is the side of Purdue that Tucker threw himself into.

After a few years of getting his feet wet at school and of working odd jobs and internships to save money, Tucker began traveling to Chicago to see a therapist who specialized in gender identity issues. Once he arrived at Purdue he had started researching all the ways that he could make himself more masculine and he had learned about hormones and surgery options, though information on both was still hard to come by in those days before the proliferation of the internet. He had done enough research on his own to know that therapy was the first necessary step in the transition process. There was no way to get around it if he ever wanted to take male hormones or have surgeries. Tucker was never a conflicted person, though, and he was very driven towards his goals of having a career and transitioning to being a man. Therapy was just one more hoop to jump through.

Between working to pay for therapy, taking classes, and traveling to Chicago frequently, Tucker didn't have much of a social life in college. His main social outlet was attending a weekly gathering of role playing game enthusiasts. Tucker wasn't quite as geeky as the other gamers, but he enjoyed being able to play the part of male characters in the games. Also, the gamers tended to come more from the serious student side of Purdue rather than the football side. Tucker was the only "woman" who attended the weekly sessions other than an odd girl named Betty who always wore purple and was obsessed with Star Trek.

Tucker liked the gamers because they were funny, self-deprecating, and smart, but guys whose intelligence had, for most of their lives, relegated them to social awkwardness. In short, they were nerds, but perfectly pleasant people. They were certainly nicer people than the frat boys and the trophy girlfriends who inhabited the "other" part of Purdue.

One of the gamers stood out to Tucker. Doug. He joined the gaming group at the end of their sophomore year. Doug was an attractive guy and he had a certain social grace that the others lacked. Tucker had seen Doug in many of his classes, because Doug was also an actuarial student, but Tucker hadn't talked to him much. When Doug started coming to gaming night, he and Tucker hit it off right away. They got each other's jokes, and practically finished each other's sentences.

In a logical world Doug and Tucker, then Sarah to the rest of the world, probably would have started dating. But their lives and their relationship was more complicated than that. Tucker, knowing from a young age that he was really a man, was focusing his romantic interest on women. Prior to meeting Sarah, Doug had never known a lesbian before. Because they got along so well as friends, though, Doug quickly seemed to accept that Sarah was gay. The two never spoke about the topic, but they related to each other completely as two men. They were brothers.

Besides, Doug had plenty of women to keep him busy as he was something of a ladies man. He had a habit of serial monogamy. He seemed to love conquest. He would fall for some girl quickly and completely, pursue her, and get her. Invariably, however, within a matter of months his attentions would turn to a new girl. He wasn't a cheater, but he was a man who always had a backup plan. One relationship would end and there was another already lined up and ready to start. Doug was not a man who spent very much time single.

Each time that Doug came to the end of a relationship, it was Tucker who was there to console him. And the next week, when Doug had someone new, Tucker would defend him to their female classmates who would grouse about the sudden turnabout. Some of Tucker's favorite times were, ironically, the night before Doug would break up with someone. The two of them would get drunk together and talk about women until all hours of the night. With their guards let down due to the alcohol, Doug might lay his head in Tucker's lap and Tucker would run his fingers through Doug's hair lovingly. On a few occasions, they fell asleep in each other's arms. The next morning, though, Doug was on to the next conquest, Tucker was back to obsessing about his gender transition plans, and they were back to being brothers again.

Tucker hated living on campus, so it wasn't long before Doug and Tucker got an apartment together off campus. It beat the hell out of the women's dorm. Tucker never felt comfortable there, though years later Doug would tease him about giving up a good thing. Doug's current girlfriend was always suspicious of him living with a chick, but Tucker was usually gone on the weekends, so he made up a story about having a girlfriend back home to help take the heat off of Doug. Little did those girls know that the woman that they knew as Sarah was 120 miles away picking up women in Chicago as a man named Tucker. The girls needn't have worried, since the only thing safer than Doug's roommate being a lesbian was him being a straight man.

Not that Tucker ever let on to Doug about his gender identity, at least, not in college. Six months after graduation Doug looked up his buddy Sarah Buchanan in the new Society of Actuaries directory, only to find her name absent. He called and got Tucker's phone number from his mom in Goshen. And when he picked up the phone that night Tucker didn't know whether to be thrilled or terrified.

Of course, since they had been so close, Doug had suspected. Things had gotten sort of weird senior year. Tucker had gotten a little more distant. Sure, they were both really busy with school, but it seemed like something was going on. Sarah had started taking testosterone over the summer before senior year, and by graduation was well on his way to becoming Tucker, though his inability to grow significant facial hair kept the transition from being overly obvious. Doug noticed Sarah was changing, but he didn't really understand. He didn't know it was possible. So he stayed silent, except to defend his friend when an occasional idiot would make a rude comment about the changes.

Doug didn't ask for details when Tucker told him he had transitioned, but just took the change on faith.

Doug worked in St. Louis for several years after graduation and Tucker and he would meet up on a regular basis in either St. Louis or Chicago to party together on a weekend. They also took at least one vacation together each year. They both could hold their share of alcohol and they had a great time women watching together. Occasionally one of them would actually pick up a woman during their outings together, but mostly they just enjoyed each other's company. One night they were battling each other for the affection of a woman that they both thought they could "bag". Each one tried to drink the other under the table so that they could take the girl. Of course, they ended up both passing out and the woman left in disgust.

Three years ago that all changed when Doug met Allison. Doug and Allison hit it off, and Doug's party days were numbered. There was an engagement and a marriage, and they moved back to Allison's hometown of Boston. Tucker was happy for his friend, and he liked Allison just fine, but he knew that his friendship with Doug was over.

Tucker grabbed his third beer from the fridge and noticed it was the last one. *Damn, I should have stopped at the liquor store.* Tucker wished that Doug was around to help him pick a new bar. Doug was always good at picking a place with hot women. He headed back to the living room and turned off the TV. He put his new copy of John Wesley Harding's *adam's apple* into the CD player and pressed play. He had put off buying it for almost two years, but had bought it on a whim last week. The last few discs of his hadn't been that good, but this one was a nice mix of the old folksy Wes, good production, and, of course, that sarcastic sense of humor.

Tucker glanced at the compact baby grand piano in the corner. He hadn't played it in longer than he could remember. He had read once that math and music were linked, and that people who were good at one tended to be good at the other. He couldn't deny that the two things that had always made the most sense to him in his life were math and music. The piano lessons that his wonderful mother had started him on at age six were really only supplementary to the natural talent and affinity that he had for the instrument.

The piano and math weren't the only things that Tucker had a natural affinity for, though. Tucker started drinking when he was about 19 years old. Family history and childhood insomnia induced by teenaged brothers who were regularly missing in action in the middle of the night, causing Tucker's parents unending stress, had lead him to resolve, early in life, that he would never be someone who abused alcohol. When he was a little kid his dad used to let him drink the last dregs of his can of Budweiser and he was allowed a glass of jug wine at Thanksgiving and Christmas meals. Other than that, his lips did not touch alcohol until college. In high school he was a teetotaler and a bit zealous about it really.

Tucker wasn't an obnoxious drinker in school, he was too focused on his studies and his transition. He wasn't the type to go out on a drinking bender. He was more of a quiet, steady drinker. Tucker was anxious to get on with his life and he was nervous on a very basic level that all of his well laid plans might fall through. So he drank to quiet his mind.

After school, alcohol began to become more and more a part of Tucker's life. His body chemistry, ingrained by genetics, easily met the challenge. He had natural tolerance. The stress of trying to be accepted as a man in the conservative environment of his actuarial jobs soon led him to drink more days than not.

Tucker would drink also to build up the confidence to try and pick up women. Tucker was not so much interested in dating women, but he got a sense of personal reassurance from being able to pick them up. He especially liked picking up straight women who might never even realize that he was transgendered. It was like a huge shot in the arm, a boost to his sense of male self.

And then, several months back, he had been angrily rejected by a woman when she discovered his transgender status. Normally, this wasn't a problem. Unbelievably, often women had no idea that Tucker was transgendered, even though he did not have a penis. Sometimes women were thrilled to simply accept oral sex or digital stimulation from Tucker.

Other times, when penetration was in order, Tucker would use a high quality prosthetic penis that attached to his body with medical grade adhesive. In a dark room, Tucker would undertake the enterprise quickly, perhaps by just unzipping, but not removing his pants. Often, a quick rendezvous of this sort left the women feeling like they were living out their favorite romance novel, and they rarely asked questions when Tucker zipped his pants back up after the encounter. Those were the straight women.

Straight women dated Tucker because he was charming and attentive. The lesbians were another story all together. Because Tucker presented as a man, picking up a lesbian for sex was usually predicated on the mutual understanding that he was transsexual. Lesbians, on the whole, were more open minded about gender-queerness, which made pickups less stressful. Though the risk of disclosure was, thus, gone with lesbians, Tucker didn't really like sleeping with them. These were the women who most often asked for second dates. And Tucker couldn't help but feel like the lesbians were using *him* for a conquest, rather than the other way around. Lesbians dated Tucker because they were intrigued by his transsexual status.

Unfortunately, the lesbians who were most likely to seek his company, femmes, Tucker had no real attraction to. Tucker valued masculinity too much, and so he found himself more sexually attracted to butches than to femmes. The straight women that he had sex with were a way for him to prove his masculinity. He would sleep with them and with femme lesbians to boost his self-confidence and self-image. Tucker's physical attraction to butches confused him, and so he tried to ignore it. Besides, those women weren't interested in sleeping with him anyway. He wrote it off that maybe he felt some sort of kinship with butch women.

He didn't let himself think about it, but Tucker was also somewhat *afraid* to be with butch women. He had decided early on that genital reconstruction surgery was too primitive and too risky. He desperately wanted a penis, because he felt it would make him a more complete man, but the chance of the surgery not going well or the results being less than satisfactory were unacceptable to Tucker.

There was another reason that he didn't want bottom surgery, but he was barely even conscious of that other reason. Tucker was still able to receive sexual pleasure from his female genitals, and he would masturbate regularly with them. He never shared this part of his sex life with others, though, because he felt it made him less of a man. As long as it was a secret that he kept to himself, a mere method of physical release that had no greater meaning attached to it, he could reconcile the disconnect between being a man and getting pleasure from his female genitals. But he knew that a butch woman would want to touch him there, and that was unacceptable. He wasn't going to be anyone's woman.

He did secretly mourn the inability to have genital pleasure with a partner, and he would often fantasize about being vaginally or anally penetrated or having his clitoris, to him his penis, manipulated. He was too afraid of what this desire meant to his manhood to share his interest with anyone, though.

Maybe that night that the woman discovered that Tucker was transgendered had happened because he was getting careless or bored. Also, it seemed that the thrill of the conquest of women didn't interest him as much anymore. He couldn't decide, though, if he wanted something emotionally deeper, or if he just wanted to be left to himself.

Chapter 20

Alec continued to obsess about Tucker for a few more days. Eventually, he couldn't bear it any longer. One evening, he got done at his job site on the south side and took the L downtown. On the ride over, he could hardly believe what he was doing. It was pretty crazy to show up at a stranger's workplace, but he felt like he had to talk to this mysterious transman.

By the time that he got there, it was 6:45. He got off the train and walked down the street a few blocks to the big office building. He entered the building and took the elevator to the floor listed in the contact information on the Terrin Power website. Odds were that it was too late. And anyway, what would Alec do if he found Tucker? *What a stupid idea!*

As long as he was here, though, he might as well see if he could find Tucker. Alec got out of the elevator on the correct floor. He crossed the hall and put his hand out to open the big glass doors of the office. *Damn...locked.* The lights in the office were still on, though, and Alec could tell that people were still working. He waited around for about ten minutes until someone opened the door on his way home. Alec rushed to go in the open door.

"Can I help you?" a portly, balding man asked Alec.

Alec froze. "Uh."

"The office is closed."

Alec thought fast. "I'm here to meet my Uncle Tucker. Tucker Buchanan. I forgot to bring my cell phone to call him to open the door."

"Oh." Without another word, the man held the door open for Alec and then headed to the elevator.

The carpeted office was full of cubicles. Alec began checking cubicles one by one for Tucker's. Halfway through the left side of the room, Alec rounded a cubicle corner and promptly ran into a man in a suit, his face hitting the man squarely directly below the knot in his tie. Before Alec could collect himself and make up a new excuse for snooping through the cubicles, the man said, "Is there something I can help you with?"

Alec gathered himself together, prepared to recite the uncle story, and realized suddenly that he had just run into Tucker.

Tucker furrowed his brow in faint recognition. "Hey, where do I know you from? I know...aren't you that kid from the grocery store the other night? What the hell are you doing here?" Tucker asked.

"Uh, yeah, that was me," Alec answered. "I, uh, wanted to talk to you."

"You're here to see *me*? How did you find out where I worked?"

"The internet is a frightening thing."

"So what's that make you, some kind of stalker or something?"

Tucker seemed irritated. "What the hell do you want?"

"I just, when I saw you the other night...what you said...did I hear you right?"

Tucker's tone softened from irritation to sarcasm. "You went to all this trouble to ask my opinion about supplements? Geez kid, I'm not some sort of naturopath."

"A what?"

"Never mind. Listen, you haven't mugged me yet, so if you've got something to say, I guess you might as well talk to me. But not here. Come on, walk me to my car, " Tucker said as he started walking towards the office doors.

Alec followed Tucker to the elevator and got in. After a few silent uncomfortable moments in the elevator, Tucker said, "So?"

Having attained his goal unexpectedly easily, Alec was at a loss as to what to say.

Tucker sighed heavily, "Look. I'm no gender counselor, kid. You're obviously on the juice, so you must be working with someone. What do you want from me? Cologne recommendations?"

Alec was silent.

"Oh...wait...you're not a fag are you? Is that what this is about? Sorry, man, I like the ladies."

"No, I mean...me too. I just...I've never met anyone else like me," Alec finally replied.

"Oh, Jesus." Tucker threw his head back and rolled his eyes.

The elevator doors opened and Tucker stepped out and headed towards a yellow sportscar in the corner.

"Is that your car?" Alec asked.

"Yeah, well, a man's got to have nice things," Tucker answered. "I don't know what to tell you, kid. Go find some guys your own age who have time to kibitz about all of the ups and downs of the human condition. Good luck, have a nice life."

Tucker stepped into his car, started the engine, and backed out, leaving Alec standing next to his empty parking space.

Alec returned home dejectedly. The only other transmen that he had ever met were from the FTM support group. Dr. Taffe had told Alec that he would need a lot of support through his transition. She had given him the contact with the FTM support group in Chicago. For a long while, Alec had been a lurker on the listserv that the group maintained. He finally attended a group meeting, but was disappointed.

He had given the group a second chance by attending a social outing with the group a few months later. One late summer day Alec met the group at Wrigley Field for a Cubs game. It was a group of about eight folks between the ages of 20 and 28. A few were in various stages of their transition, but most identified as "genderqueer". Alec was excited to meet others who were going through what he was going through, but most of the folks in the group seemed more interested in talking about their own lives and problems than in helping someone else. Also, to working class Alec, many of them seemed young and spoiled. They talked about using their student loans to have surgery, or about how to tell their parents about their situation. Alec had never even had a chance to finish high school, much less go to college. And whether or not his parents accepted him as a FTM was the least of his problems. He hadn't even spoken to his family in nearly ten years. No one from the listserv seemed to be anything like Alec. Even worse, none of them seemed to have their shit together any better than Alec did. It seemed like a classic case of the blind leading the blind.

So Alec continued to read the listserv for hints and recommendations on various topics of interest to him in his transition, but he was hesitant to hang out with the members of the group again. And so he didn't. He just didn't identify with their experiences.

By no stretch of the imagination did Alec identify with Tucker's seemingly expensive, upper-class lifestyle either, but Tucker did seem like a man who had his life together. He didn't seem confused or ambiguous. He was a confident, adult male. Without a doubt, he was a real man. Alec admired that quality in Tucker. Tucker, unlike the folks in the FTM group, had come out on the other side of his transition and was truly living his life as a man, rather than some sort of transitional man.

And Alec longed for a friend to talk to. Smitty was out of the picture, and where she went, so went Gail. The people at work couldn't care less. Jessie's friends were idiots. Even Jessie was starting to seem like she didn't understand what Alec was going through. He found it harder and harder to talk to her about his transition.

Without many other options, and suddenly fascinated and obsessed with Tucker, Alec decided that he had to get to know Tucker. He began to go down to Terrin Power several times to wait for Tucker beside his parking spot. The first time that Alec did this, Tucker noted his presence, shook his head sadly, and headed into the elevator to his office. Tucker didn't want to encourage the behavior, and figured that Alec would get the hint and stop coming.

Chapter 21

Tucker knew that he was no role model. He figured that this kid was better off without his guidance. Plus, Tucker had never been a fan of forming close ties with anyone. He figured it was better for all involved if he just kept to himself.

Besides, Tucker had more to worry about than whether some baby-tranny was stalking him. Things at work were starting to go sour. It was a perennial problem for Tucker. The insurance companies and actuarial firms that Tucker had worked for his entire career were typically conservative workplaces. Tucker had been easily passing as a man since the time of his first real job at age 22, but it didn't make things any easier. Tucker found that his independent nature tended to get him in trouble.

He often thought, usually correctly so, that he was smarter than his supervisors, and he was frustrated by their unimaginative approaches to projects. Tucker was also a rabid liberal and a health food nut, while he found that his coworkers were usually flag waving Republicans who couldn't go a day in life without red meat, soda, or potato chips. And forget exercise.

Tucker worshiped his own body, the only toxin he ever put in it being alcohol. His vegetarian, whole grain lunches and his bulging biceps were out of place amongst the baloney on white bread and potbellies. The guys at work would talk about the NASCAR race that they saw on TV the weekend before, or how their wives were nagging them all the time about this or that. They dripped mustard from their lunches on their ties and hardly bothered to wipe it off. The slightly higher class ones would blather for hours about playing golf. It made Tucker angry that he had to work hard every day of his life to be able to express his masculinity, while he saw the men around him lazily taking it for granted. He thought that his coworkers were pigs who were wasting the glorious bodies that they'd been granted at birth.

Tucker was the embodiment of the GQ man. He was good looking, he dressed impeccably, he was smart, and he had incredible social grace. His social grace, though, like so many other things about Tucker, was a means to an end. He didn't want to be considered an odd duck, or have his gender identity questioned, so he learned early in life to be charming. He took his cue from the Dale Carnegie school of manners: if you pretend that you like other people and that they are important, they will like you back. So Tucker made superficial friendships easily. He was quick with a handshake or a slap on the back. He laughed at everyone's jokes and always had a smile on his face. This persona was a façade, though, that covered his nearly universal contempt for other people. Tucker was a loner at heart, a hopeless introvert, who often felt that he had to play the gregarious role just to get by under the radar.

Periodically, he found the pressure to perform, to be constantly "on" at work to be too much. He would lash out at a coworker in contempt, or withdraw entirely into himself. Often, his most acidic words were reserved for his supervisors, who often tried to belittle him because they felt threatened by his intelligence and creativity. These small, frequent slights would build up in Tucker's subconscious, until he would finally lose it and quit.

Tucker had fallen into such a period at Terrin Power, and he was concerned with how much longer he would be able to stay in the job. Since he graduated college, Tucker had been through about five jobs in 16 years. He was approaching the start of his fifth year at Terrin Power, and he could almost hear the time bomb ticking. He was forever amazed that he was able to get new jobs based on recommendations from former employers, but the truth was that, for all of his personal foibles, Tucker was an extremely intelligent person, a hard, no-nonsense worker, and a more than competent actuary. However threatened Tucker's strengths made his employers feel, he also made or saved them a great deal of money.

Compounding his troubles at work, Tucker's social life was getting stale. Tucker had never had a steady girlfriend in his life, but chose instead to primarily pick up strangers in bars for one-night stands. Occasionally a woman would stick around for a second date or third, but Tucker actually preferred not to see them again. He liked his time alone and didn't like having to emotionally interact with someone on a long-term basis. He was usually successful in hooking up with someone once or twice a month, and he found this sufficient. In recent years, though, the one-night stands began to wear on Tucker. It took a lot of energy to pick up a woman in a bar and take her home. For many years, the thrill of the pickup and the pleasure of the sex was enough to sustain him. But he found more and more that the enterprise was beginning to disappoint him.

The rest of his social time he spent mostly in bars that catered to businessmen, drinking martinis and talking to the bartenders or doormen. Tucker found it easy to interact with these service workers. They appreciated his Dale Carnegie approach, and he, in turn, appreciated their hard working, hard drinking lifestyles. They seemed to be more genuinely masculine men than the wimps that he felt he worked with. In spite of his conversations with service workers, though, since his best friend Doug had gotten married and moved to Boston three years ago, he hadn't really found anyone else who was worth much effort.

Tucker took his comfort in his daily two-hour workout regimen, in the nice things that he owned, and in his drinking. Periodically, he would take up the piano again, but that hadn't been the case for a number of years now. For a long time, these things were enough for him. But lately the conflicts at work and the constant carousing had begun to wear on him. He felt bored and tired and, though he would never admit it to himself or to anyone else, maybe just a little bit lonely.

When Alec began showing up at his parking spot Tucker wasn't so much annoyed as amused. He outwardly ignored Alec, but he couldn't help but feel a little bit flattered. Tucker himself had never sought out the company of other FTMs. He preferred to observe "factory direct" men and take cues from the best of their collection. He wondered what Alec saw in him that seemed to have grabbed his attention so completely. He wondered if maybe someone could see that he wasn't such a bad guy after all.

Chapter 22

Tucker stepped out of the elevator into the parking garage. Not surprisingly, for the third day in a row, he found Alec leaning against a concrete pillar not far from the Ghia.

"We've got to stop meeting like this, kid," Tucker said as he threw his briefcase into the car. Tucker looked at Alec and for the first time he felt a little sorry for him as Alec stood there with a sheepish smile on his face and his hands stuck in his pockets. "What do I have to do to get you to stop wasting your life in this parking garage?"

"You could talk to me," Alec said.

Tucker let out a big sigh. It had to be a bad idea, but he had to give the kid credit for persistence. "One drink, but don't make me regret this," he said to Alec. "Hop in, and don't get any mud on the floor."

Alec's heart jumped and he diligently knocked the dried spring mud off of his boots and got in the passenger side of the beautiful yellow car.

"You ARE 21, right? I don't want to get busted for corrupting a minor," Tucker said as they exited the parking garage.

"Yeah, of course, I'm 24. Well, I will be in the fall, anyway."

"Oh, practically on social security, then." Tucker's condescending comments cut Alec, but he was so happy to finally be talking to Tucker he tried to let it pass.

Tucker sensed that Alec was hurt, and so he tried to be friendlier. "So, what's your pleasure, cowboy? What kind of places do you go to?"

"Mostly, dyke bars up in Andersonville where I live."

"Dykes. They're awfully high maintenance. Besides, I'm not turning this drink into a field trip to the outer banks. Let's go to a regular bar. You ought to be able to pass by now."

Tucker spotted a parking spot on the street and nabbed it. "We've got a few blocks to walk, but I know a nice place."

A misty rain was falling, but it was a nice night out. Tucker turned up the collar on his overcoat and Alec put up the hood on his rain jacket. They turned in under an awning and Tucker opened a large dark wood door with brass fixtures.

They passed overstuffed chairs occupied by men in suits smoking cigars and laughing deeply as they took small sips from their single malt scotch on the rocks. They headed to the empty bar stools and sat down.

After a few moments a middle-aged bartender came over to them. "Hey, Tucker, haven't seen you in here for a few weeks."

"Yeah, well, a man's got to spread the wealth, ya know? Jeff, I want you to meet an acquaintance of mine." Tucker turned to Alec and realized he didn't know his name.

"I'm Alec."

"Well, Alec, what will you have?"

"Miller Lite."

"And your regular, Tuck?"

"Certainly."

The bartender put a martini glass on the counter and filled it with ice. He swung around and grabbed a shiny silver shaker and put a scoop of ice in it. Next he took a tall frosty bottle marked Belvedere in one hand and a plastic bottle with a spout in the other and began to pour each into the shaker. After a moment he set aside the plastic bottle and continued pouring with the other hand. He placed the top on the shaker and began to shake it violently for what seemed like a lifetime. Alec was mesmerized by the pageantry of the process and watched intently. Eventually, the bartender set down the shaker, opened a green bottle and poured a small amount of its contents over the ice in the glass. He swirled the glass and dumped the ice out into the sink. He resumed shaking for a moment, removed the top of the shaker and strained its contents into the frosty glass. He filled the glass to the very brim, so that it seemed for sure that some would spill out the top. The bartender then grabbed three large, green olives, skewered them, and placed them in the glass. He opened a door under the bar and produced a frosted pilsner glass. From behind yet another door he brought out a bottle of Miller Lite. He opened the bottle and set the empty glass and the bottle in front of Alec, and then returned with the martini.

"A tab, Tuck?" the bartender said as he poured Alec's beer into the glass.

"No, we're just having one tonight," Tucker replied.

"Fourteen dollars even."

Alec, reeling in his mind over the cost of the two drinks, reached for his wallet, but Tucker grabbed his arm to stop him as he set a twenty dollar bill on the counter in front of him and nodded an unspoken communication to the bartender.

"Thank ya, sir," the bartender said and respectfully disappeared to the other end of the bar. Alec waited for him to return with change, but he didn't, and Tucker didn't seem to notice.

Tucker took a sip of his martini without lifting it from the bar and said, "You wanted to talk…so talk. This is your big chance."

Alec had waited for this moment for so long, thinking about it constantly for weeks, but now that the moment had arrived, he was at a loss as to what to say.

"Well?"

"I don't know what to say. I mean. I just want to know about your life," Alec stuttered.

"Well, detective, you've been following me for a week or more, I suspect you already know a fair amount about my life."

"I mean, how did you get here?" Alec said.

"Ah, you want to know the gory details. You don't really need to hear about that. It's all ancient history. Besides, you seem to be on track. You've been on the stuff, what, 8 months?"

"It will be a year in June."

"Yeah, so, you're on your way. So the details aren't important. Just get there. And then don't look back. I haven't. And I don't really care to."

The two of them sat in uncomfortable silence, drinking their drinks. Tucker fit well into the setting. He was younger than the rest of the crowd, but he blended in easily. He was just another suit. No one took any special notice of him. Alec gazed at the remarkable person sitting next to him as Tucker looked straight ahead. He was incredibly handsome and well put together. His hair was trimmed impeccably, his clothes tailored perfectly. Alec noticed just a few very short gray hairs above Tucker's ear.

Tucker began to settle into his first drink fog. He loved that moment when he began to feel the impact of the alcohol. A sudden wash of relaxation mixed with a very small loss of self-consciousness.

Tucker was impressed with Alec's persistence. He certainly hadn't given Alec any reason to continue pursuing contact, and yet here they were. Tucker was good at reading people. Alec was young, but Tucker could see some complicated things in Alec's eyes. In spite of himself, he was oddly curious what the kid's story was. Tucker had very high standards for men, both in terms of their actions and their appearance. Alec was relatively early yet in his transition, but he looked good. He seemed physically strong and he had abundant and well-groomed facial hair. His appearance was obviously important to him, which Tucker found admirable. What little Tucker knew of Alec, he could tell that he was very genuine. He had the makings of a good man, he was just a little shy and unsure of himself. If Tucker knew anything, it was how to project confidence.

Finally, halfway through his martini, Tucker said, "Don't you know anybody else, or are you just trapped amongst the lesbos in Andersonville?"

"You're the first person I've seen out in real life."

"Geez, kid, it's Chicago for chrissakes. And you obviously know how to use the internet."

"Yeah, I know there's a group. I went once, but I just didn't fit in there. They were too different from me. It was too hard."

"Oh, but stalking me seemed easy," Tucker answered.

"I don't know, you just seem to have all of your shit together already. You seem normal. You seem amazing." Alec embarrassed himself with this last hasty admission.

Tucker smiled and laughed to himself. *Me…normal. Me…amazing. Damn, this kid is more fucked up than I thought.*

"Finish your drink, kid. I'm gonna take you out. It's about time you started 'the real life experience.'"

Chapter 23

Tucker and Alec walked back to Tucker's car, got in and drove for about 15 minutes.

"Now look, kid. If I take you here you gotta be cool, okay? I got read by this chick a while back and it's taken me a long time to be able to go back. I don't want a repeat of that."

Alec nodded but Tucker wondered if Alec had any idea what he was talking about.

"So where are we going?" Alec said.

"It's just this place I know. Real nice middle class folks. Yuppie wanna-bes mostly. But the ladies are good looking and the men don't cause any trouble. They're all too busy trying to seem 'sensitive.'"

They were sufficiently out of the heart of the city by now that there was a surface lot next to the building that Tucker pulled up to and parked at. They got out and went up to the door. Halfway there, Tucker turned on his heels and looked Alec straight in the eye.

"Whatever doubts or insecurities that you have, fella, let 'em go right now, right here in this parking lot. Stand up straight. Hold your head up. You are more of a man than most of those losers in there will ever be. You have to believe that."

Tucker was taking a big chance by bringing Alec here. It was the first time that he had been back since the incident last year. In all of his 39 years Tucker had been lucky that most of the anti-queer incidents that he had been involved with involved words only. He had not ever been the victim of physical violence. But the situation a year ago had hovered dangerously at the edge.

The evening had begun like so many others at Friendly's. Tucker drank a martini and scoped out the crowd. He had settled on a dark-headed middle-aged woman who was sitting alone at the bar. He approached her and began a conversation.

"Would you mind a little company?" Tucker said.

"No, I wouldn't mind at all," the woman answered.

Tucker sat down at the bar next to her. "My name's Tucker."

"Oh, that's unique. I'm Michelle."

The rest of the interaction had been unremarkable. Tucker had quickly put Michelle at ease, and it wasn't long before she was talking about her divorce, her college-aged son, and her general disenchantment with the dating scene. As was Tucker's MO, he listened and made lots of direct eye contact. After a few hours, Michelle asked him if he'd like to continue their conversation back at her place.

Tucker had developed a sort of sense for picking women out of a crowd who were just lonely enough, with just low enough self esteem, that they might be likely to be extremely receptive to special attention. He avoided real charity cases, because they posed no challenge whatsoever, but he had a way of knowing which woman in a room was just teetering on the edge of desperation, but who hadn't quite fallen off that edge yet. Michelle seemed like a textbook case.

The two of them drove their separate cars back to Michelle's place. They started, as these things normally would, by having another drink. Tucker commented that Michelle looked a little tense and would she like a back rub. Michelle had accepted. Tucker used his strong hands to apply gentle, but firm pressure to Michelle's back for about ten minutes. And then he had started to kiss her gently on the neck.

One thing led to another, Michelle's clothes had disappeared, and Tucker's mouth had found it's way to most of the nooks and crannies of Michelle's body while he had managed to remove only his own shirt. Ordinarily Tucker would have been very sure to dim the lights before intimate contact began, but for some reason he had neglected to do so on this particular occasion.

As things got more intense, it became apparent that Michelle wanted to have intercourse. Things were moving too fast and Tucker didn't have time to prepare. Tucker began to put together in his mind how to present the impotency story that he would normally tell when trapped in such a situation where disclosure seemed a possibility. Before he could get the words out, though, Michelle suddenly shoved her hand down his pants. He couldn't manage to wiggle away in time, and Michelle's hand passed across his merkin and the prosthesis. Though the dildo looked and functioned realistically enough, it did not feel like real flesh.

Michelle withdrew her hand from Tucker's pants quickly. "What the hell is that?"

It wasn't the first time this had ever happened. And though Tucker wasn't pleased that the encounter had come to this climax, he also wasn't overly concerned yet.

"I should have said something sooner. I'm sorry. I have a genetic disorder." Tucker felt that the last statement was absolutely accurate, though the two preceding statements were not accurate representations of his feelings in the least.

The normal progression of things at this point would be sympathy from the woman. She might ask questions, or she might let it go, but either way she would normally feel badly for Tucker. If pressed, Tucker would explain that he had been born with a very small penis and that he made up for it with the dildo, which again, to his mind was completely true. And sometimes the sexual encounter would end and Tucker would receive unwanted pity. But usually there was no conflict over the topic.

On that fateful night, though, there would be no sex nor sympathy. The seed of suspicion had been planted in Michelle and so Tucker never got a chance to trot out his genetic defect story. It seemed by her reaction that Michelle was just smart enough and just paranoid enough to have suddenly put a number of factors together in her head. Perhaps Tucker's relatively slight stature for a man, the faint scars on his chest, and yes, even his uncharacteristic charm.

Before Tucker could answer Michelle's question, Michelle offered her own explanation. "Oh my god. What kind of freak are you? You're a fucking dyke, aren't you?" Michelle jumped up and grabbed her shirt and panties and frantically began to get dressed.

"Michelle, just calm down. Let's talk this out."

"Fuck you, you freak. You misled me." Michelle's voice was

starting to get louder and more shrill.

"I'm just going to go." Tucker said, sensing that the situation was deteriorating fast. He grabbed his shirt and his shoes and began to put them on.

By now, Michelle was dressed except for her shoes. "You *better* fucking get the hell out of my house! How could you do this to me? How could you rape me? I ought to call the cops."

Whoa. Rape? Tucker decided that his shoes and shirt were less important than getting the hell out of there fast. He got up, grabbed his keys off of the side table and his suit coat off of a nearby chair, and headed for the door.

Michelle grabbed one of her high heel shoes off of the floor and hurled it at Tucker while screaming, "You fucker!" The shoe hit Tucker squarely in the back of the head, though luckily with the blunt end rather than the heel.

Tucker didn't bother turning back. He slammed the door behind him and rushed to his car, which was parked several blocks down the street. Michelle followed him out to the sidewalk, screaming incoherently at him the entire time. He got to his car, got in, and drove off. Michelle ran out into the street after him and managed to bang her hands on the back end of the car before he could get away.

The situation had been more than unpleasant. It had been frightening. It had kept him away from Friendly's for a good long time and also away from straight girls.

Tucker knew that if things went badly tonight at the bar, it would probably scar Alec for life. And besides, they might just get their asses kicked.

But, suddenly, for some reason, Tucker really wanted to show Alec how his life could be. He wanted to show Alec that he could really be a man. That he could function in the real world and not just be relegated to the lesbian ghetto. Besides, meeting Alec and receiving his obvious admiration had given Tucker a shot in the arm. It made him feel like puffing out his chest. He had hidden from his favorite pickup joint for too long and for all the wrong reasons. It was time that he reclaimed it. In a weird way, Alec motivated him to be strong again.

They entered the bar and were stopped at the entrance by a man of about age 40 who asked for their IDs.

"Do I look that young, Ray?" Tucker asked.

"Hey, Tuck! Long time no see! Jesus, to what do we owe the honor?" the doorman said while grabbing Tucker's right hand and shaking firmly and slapping him on the back with his other hand.

"Oh, you know, I had to give the women in the rest of the city a shot at me, but I always return for quality."

"Damn right. Shit, there are some hot twats in here tonight too. I wish that I wasn't working."

"Patience, my good man, all shifts must end sometime."

"Ain't that the truth?"

Alec observed the interaction intently. It was obvious that Tucker was well liked and that others accepted him as a man.

"Ray, this is my buddy, Alec," Tucker said as he pulled Alec into the room by the shoulder. Even with the nice beard that he had coming in, Alec had a baby face that well warranted an ID check. Tucker guessed that the gender on Alec's driver's license was likely still female, and he wanted to avoid the possibility of disclosure, even though he guessed that Ray wouldn't notice.

"Hey, Alec, good to meet you," Ray said enthusiastically as he shook Alec's hand.

Tucker moved forward, pulling on Alec's elbow as he went. "Good to see you, Ray. Take it easy. Pace yourself until closing time."

"Yes sir, I will do that."

Having successfully avoided the ID check, Tucker took Alec up to the bar with him. Alec, oblivious to Tucker's calculated and purposeful handling of the doorman, followed Tucker in a self-conscious haze.

The two of them stayed at the bar until closing time. Tucker pointed out women to Alec who were likely marks and bought a few of them drinks and made playful banter with them.

Alec watched Tucker in fascination. Tucker had all of the classic male physical moves down. The way that he walked, the way that he used his hands, the cadence of his speech. When he was with a woman Tucker took his moves from a page of the old style gentleman's book. He was entirely charming. At the same time, though, Tucker had the benefit of growing up in the world being perceived as female. So he knew how men belittle women. He used this knowledge to his advantage. He let the women talk. He let the women tell him their stories. He didn't rush matters to get to the prize at the end of the evening.

Ironically, Tucker didn't enjoy the company of women that much. From the youngest age he had been fixated on the trappings and manner of the male world. And, in fact, both men and women disappointed him again and again. No woman could ever match up to the standard that his mother had set early in his life. And no man could ever match up to the ideal man that Tucker had constructed in his mind, the man that he aspired to be. These ridiculous standards set Tucker up for disappointment and unhappiness time and time again.

At 2am Tucker and Alec left the bar. On the way out Tucker stepped over to where Ray, the doorman, was putting chairs on top of tables. He whispered something in Ray's ear and motioned with his head towards a table of women who were gathering their things and getting ready to leave. Ray smiled at Tucker and nodded, and as Tucker turned to rejoin Alec, Ray headed over to the table and started talking to the women.

Tucker drove Alec home to Andersonville. He had made a point of not getting too shit-faced tonight so that he would be in his best form to show Alec "how it's done". Alec seemed tired, unaccustomed as he was to staying up late, and overwhelmed. Alec had called Jessie around 10pm to warn her that he would be home late, but he hadn't expected that the evening would drag on quite this long. Tucker dropped off Alec and they said goodnight. Alec closed the car door and began to walk away. Before Alec disappeared into his building, Tucker leaned across the passenger seat and rolled down the window.

"Hey kid!" Tucker called.

Alec turned around.

"Nice job in there tonight. I think the ladies liked you."

Alec smiled and looked down at his feet and blushed. He waved off Tucker and went inside his building.

Driving home Tucker felt good, better than he had in a while. There was something entertaining about guiding Alec through the manly ways of the world. It was a position that Tucker had never found himself in before: mentor. He was unaccustomed to people relying on him, but he kind of liked the way that Alec seemed to want to depend on him as a guide.

Chapter 24

Walking into his building, Alec was touched and overwhelmed by Tucker's words. He had wanted to hug him at the end of the night for taking him under his wing, but he knew that was the wrong thing to do. A year ago, Tucker's words would have brought Alec to tears, but testosterone had already begun to eliminate crying from Alec's emotional spectrum.

But he couldn't stop smiling. He didn't care if the ladies liked him, and in fact he was certain that his shy silence prevented anyone at the bar that night from taking much note of him. But Tucker's approval, now that was something to be proud of. And so Alec, instead, took Tucker's words to heart and became determined not to let this amazing man down.

Alec was used to passing as a man by now, but he didn't often challenge himself with new situations. It was pretty easy to pass at worksites because everyone women were so unusual at construction sites. Plus, people were always too busy to snoop into each other's personal lives. Socially, Alec stuck to the safe atmosphere of Andersonville and its accepting population of lesbians. Mostly he spent his social time with Jessie, either at Club 69 or at home. Jessie's friends all knew Alec's situation and he was rarely challenged on his status. Alec avoided doing things socially with the FTM group, because so many of them seemed to have problems that it depressed him to hang out with them. And none of them seemed like real men to Alec, either, which was a painful reminder of the nagging feeling that he had that he might not be measuring up as a man. Tucker was so dramatically different than anyone in the FTM group. He was undeniably a man. And he was so confident and successful.

The trip to this unknown straight bar was way out of Alec's comfort zone. He had felt simultaneously thrilled and terrified. He did his best not to let his fear show and he watched Tucker intently all night for cues as to how to behave.

Alec continued to be amazed by this man who had gone through transition and come out successful. Normal. He admired and cared for him so much. He observed his every action like he was studying for an exam. Indeed he was, he was studying for life, his final exam for becoming a man. Alec knew that Tucker had issues. He obviously drank too much and he was a little bit full of himself. But Alec didn't hold these small transgressions against Tucker. Alec knew as well as anyone that sometimes we all have to do whatever we can to get through life.

Alec sensed that night was the beginning of more than a mentor-student relationship, though. Alec thought that he and Tucker were oddly complementary to each other. They were both introverts, no doubt about that, but they exhibited the trait in entirely different ways. Tucker was seemingly gregarious and open to other people, but mentally and emotionally withdrawn at a deeper level. Alec was quiet and slow to open up to others, but he connected with other people better once he got to know them and empathized with others easily. Tucker could help to show Alec how to interact with others in a more relaxed way, and Alec hoped that he'd be able to open Tucker's heart to the gifts of other people.

Chapter 25

Tucker couldn't remember the last time that he "hung out" with someone on a regular basis. It might have been in college. But he soon found that there were regular messages on his cell phone from Alec. And he felt compelled to return the calls in spite of himself.

Alec gave Tucker someone to talk to for the first time in ages. Though they were separated by wide variations in class and education, they had a shared soul. They understood each other in a very basic way, and no topic was off limits. Tucker didn't even realize that he had been missing intimate human contact until he started to get a taste for it. Tucker was forever surprised by how smart and emotionally intuitive that Alec was even though he barely had any formal education at all. It seemed that Alec knew how to challenge Tucker on his bullshit in a way that never irritated Tucker, but instead made him really start to think about his life and his motivations.

Alec was a positive influence on Tucker in practical ways too. Alec wasn't much of a drinker, and he wasn't interested in picking up women in bars. Alec was also someone who needed a great deal of sleep and who worked long, hard days of physical labor. So Tucker began to let Alec steer him away from his hard drinking and late night carousing, and towards healthier activities.

It wasn't long before Alec was coming over to watch the most recent Netflix arrivals on a regular basis. And to Tucker's surprise, soon he was putting titles into his queue with Alec's taste in mind.

Tucker also began to take great pride in introducing Alec to the finer things in life, in particular, healthy eating. Alec wasn't much of a chef, and sustained himself on peanut butter and jelly and baloney sandwiches interspersed with whatever meat and potatoes meal that Jessie made for him. Tucker, a staunch vegetarian and health food nut, would cook healthy, vegetable laden meals for Alec, and even managed to slip in a bit of tofu every now and then. Since Tucker was a competent chef, Alec couldn't help but enjoy the strange meals.

Tucker also tried to encourage Alec to work out, and invited him to visit the gym with him periodically. Alec admitted that he was impressed with Tucker's strong, well-toned male body, and longed for the same, but said that he couldn't bring himself to work out, especially after a long, hard day on the work site.

Because Alec preferred to ride his bike for exercise, Tucker began to go on rides with him. Tucker ended up enjoying the bicycling so much, that he bought Alec a brand new bicycle so that Alec could keep up with the state of the art custom made Waterford that Tucker had recently purchased for himself up in Wisconsin.

One weekend, the two of them decided to bike together from Chicago to Milwaukee, spend the night, and bike back the next day. It was about a 100 mile trip each way. Alec told Tucker about the idea after he heard about the Frozen Snot Century, a winter ride where a group of hard-core bicyclists took the same route.

They waited until the weather warmed up, and headed out early one spring morning. Alec hadn't taken a bike trip this long since that long ride from Belleville to Chicago back when he was 14. He thought about that trip from long ago a lot during the first several miles of the trip to Milwaukee.

"This bike is a lot nicer than the one that I moved to Chicago on," Alec said after the first several miles were behind them.

"That's what money will do for you, bring you comfort," Tucker answered matter-of-factly.

"Yeah, well, I'm not used to being comfortable."

Tucker took a swig from his water bottle. "Well you better fucking get used to it kid, it won't be long before you're making the big bucks."

"What are you talking about, I'm never gonna be rich."

"I'm not talking about being rich, bitch. I'm talking about being comfortable."

Alec looked over his left shoulder to check for traffic and then swerved around a pothole that he had spotted. "It's hard for me to think that I'll ever get ahead."

Alec waited for a response for a moment, then realized that Tucker wasn't pedaling beside him any longer. Alec looked behind him and Tucker had stopped. Alec circled back to where Tucker had stopped.

"Are you okay? Did you get a flat?" Alec asked.

"I'm fine. But I'm not biking all the way to the frickin' Cream City if I gotta listen to your bellyaching the whole way."

"I'm not bellyaching," Alec protested.

Tucker held up his hand. "Stop, just stop right there." Alec stopped talking and put his hands on what testosterone had left of his hips.

"You are a winner. You have overcome all the bullshit that anyone could have thrown at them. You are going to succeed," Tucker said tersely.

Alec was taken aback by this line of conversation.

Tucker continued. "The only thing that can keep you down now is you. Don't you dare stop believing in yourself."

Alec suddenly felt embarrassed.

Tucker persisted. "Are you listening, dammit?"

"Yeah, yeah, I'm listening, stop hollering."

"Good. Now let's hurry up and get somewhere that we can stop and have lunch, I'm already starving."

They averaged about 15 miles per hour, and including the lunch stop in Racine, the ride to Milwaukee ended up taking about eight hours.

Chapter 26

Tucker and Alec began to spend a great deal of time together, usually several evenings a week and at least one day on the weekends. Often, when they weren't together, they were on the phone together.

At first, Jessie was happy that Alec had found another FTM to commiserate with. In truth, as Alec began to change more and more, Jessie knew less and less how to relate to him. She loved him deeply, but he was becoming a different person from the woman that she had started dating almost three years before.

Jessie was beginning to wonder how dating a man affected her own sexual orientation. Was she still a lesbian? Bisexual? Things were even more complicated for her because, though she would never tell Alec, deep down inside she still thought of Alec as a woman. But Alec, and the rest of the world, saw Alec as a man.

Jessie had struggled her entire life as a femme lesbian. Her sexual orientation was constantly in question. "You're too pretty to be a lesbian," men would tell her while they tried to convince her to let them buy her a drink. On the street, she was invisible as a gay person. Some people would be glad for the cover, but Jessie wasn't. It frustrated her. Part of why she liked dating butch women so much was their visibility. She admired the strength that it took to go through life as an obvious dyke. She thought it was sexy. When she was out in public with a butch lover, she was visible. Her identity became concrete.

With a passing FTM, Jessie's sexuality became invisible again. She wanted to be the kind of person who loved someone for what was inside of them, not for what was on the outside. But this was hard. Alec's changes reflected as much on Jessie's identity as it did on Alec's. Only Alec had gotten to make the decision, and Jessie just had to deal with the fallout.

Jessie thought that the irony of loving someone is that you want the best for them, but at the same time you have to be concerned about how every decision that they make affects your own life. Jessie wanted to support Alec and to love him unconditionally as a man, but the change reflected too much change on her own life to feel neutral about it.

Jessie was afraid that Alec felt that if she truly loved him, that she would accept him as a man. She was afraid to talk to him about it in part because she knew it would make him feel threatened in his fragile sense of masculinity and in part because she was afraid that she would lose him.

Chapter 27

Alec got home from work and threw his keys on the kitchen table. "Hey baby, I'm home."

"I'm in here ironing," Jessie called from the living room. Alec walked into the living room and saw several of his nicest shirts hanging from various furniture in the room.

"Hey, babe," Alec said to her as he reached out and pulled her tight to him and gave her a kiss. "Thanks for doing my shirts."

"Yeah, no problem," Jessie said.

Alec went to the bathroom and stripped off his dirty work clothes and started a hot shower. He looked at his face in the bathroom mirror while he waited for the shower to heat up. He pulled at the edges of his moustache and goatee and checked to see if he needed a clean up shave. He was disappointed to see that he didn't and that the shave from several days ago was still holding up pretty well. He loved to shave. He considered shaving anyway, even though he didn't really need it, but the mirror fogged up before he could. Instead, he stepped into the shower and lathered up with his favorite Bay Rum soap. He washed his close cut hair and let the warm water run down the back of his neck as he hung his head forward under the water. *Damn, it was hot out there today.* He soaped up a second time to be sure to get the summer sweat off.

Alec emerged from the shower and ducked into the bedroom. Much to his dismay, Jessie was lying on the bed.

"Jesus, babe, I'm not dressed," Alec said startled, as he quickly wrapped the towel in his hand around his naked body.

"That's okay by me," Jessie cooed.

Alec walked over to the window and closed the shades and then turned off the overhead light. He went over to the dresser and hurriedly searched for a shirt.

"Alec, come here."

"Let me just put something on," Alec said as he slid a white t-shirt over his head and reached for a pair of boxer shorts.

Jessie got up from the bed and stomped out of the room and into the kitchen.

"Where are you going, Jess?" Alec said as he followed her.

Jessie was visibly irritated. "Can't we just have normal sex?" she barked.

Alec was confused. "What do you mean?"

Jessie shook her head and walked out of the kitchen and into the living room, passing by Alec so closely that he had to step aside to avoid her bumping into him.

Before Alec could follow Jessie to the living room, she turned on her heels. "I mean, stone butch is one thing, but I never get to even see your body anymore." Jessie wasn't looking at Alec, but rather up at the ceiling or at the walls. Her mannerisms made it seem like she was actually talking to herself, debating herself, rather than talking to Alec.

Alec was becoming more and more comfortable with his body as testosterone helped redeposit his fat and made him more muscular. He was VERY uncomfortable with his breasts and female genitals, though. He longed for the surgical changes that would complete his transition and make him even more comfortable in his body. Jessie's gaze made him uncomfortable because it made him feel like he was still a woman.

Alec could feel the blood start to rush to his face. He looked down at his feet. Before he could say anything, Jessie continued.

"It makes me think that you must be getting it somewhere else. I bet you let Mr. Perfect fuck your brains out."

Alec's embarrassment and shame turned to surprise, and then quickly to anger. "What the fuck are you talking about?"

"Don't play all innocent with me. Jesus, all you ever talk about anymore is Tucker. If you're not with him, you're on the phone with him. I see the way you look all moony-eyed at him. I know what's going on."

"What are you, crazy? Tucker and I are just friends, you know that," Alec said emphatically.

"Yeah, *right.*" Jessie stormed back into the bedroom.

Jessie's comment infuriated Alec. Alec walked into the bedroom. "Tucker is a guy for chrissakes!"

"Yeah, well, it seems these days that all you're interested in anymore is guy stuff," Jessie replied.

Jessie pulled open the shade and stared out the window. After a moment of silence Alec said, "Fine. Believe whatever you want. You're the only person that I want to sleep with, and if you can't take my word for that I don't know what the fuck to say."

Alec stormed into the living room and grabbed a pair of his jeans and two socks from a pile of clean laundry on the couch and pulled one of his freshly ironed shirts off of a hanger. He dressed quickly, put his shoes on, grabbed his keys and wallet from the table and left the apartment, slamming the door behind him.

Alec was so angry with Jessie. His entire life he had felt weird…wrong…out of place. Finally, he felt like the puzzle pieces of his life were falling together. With each passing day on hormones he felt more and more comfortable with his body. He couldn't wait to emerge at the other end of all this change as a complete man. For the first time in his life he felt like standing more upright. He felt strong. He felt proud.

His pride in his transition was only matched by his joy in finding a kindred spirit in the world. Alec was a friendly, easy-going person, but he had never felt like he truly connected with other people. He felt like English was his second language, and that as such he was never quite able to communicate effectively with others.

But that all changed when he met Tucker. Once Tucker began to let down his guard, the connection between them was swift and complete. For the first time in his life Alec felt that someone understood him completely. He felt that he could say anything to Tucker and there would be no judgment placed on his thoughts, feelings, and ideas. Alec loved Tucker deeply, indeed more than he had ever loved anyone, but it was the love of a brother. Alec felt that Tucker was his soul mate, but he had no interest in becoming his lover.

Alec's anger at Jessie began to melt away into sadness at once more being misunderstood. Alec loved Jessie. He craved physical contact with her beautiful body. But she didn't understand how Alec could want her and love Tucker as well. Worse still, Jessie didn't understand Alec's transition. And Alec was beginning to think that Jessie didn't WANT to understand Alec's transition. He feared that what she really wanted was to be with a butch woman. And if that was what Jessie wanted, then she didn't want him. Alec wanted so badly to cry, but the tears wouldn't come. He wondered if he could ever find a woman that would love him as a man. He wanted Jessie to be that woman. But what if she wasn't?

Alec rubbed his eyes with his fists as he entered the Berwyn train stop station. He sat on a bench on the platform and tried to blank out his mind so the pain would stop as he waited to board a train headed downtown.

Chapter 28

Back at the apartment, Jessie paced angrily. She didn't understand the changes happening in Alec, but she knew that he spent all of his time when they weren't together either at work or with Tucker. She was jealous of all of the time that Alec spent with Tucker. Each time Alec mentioned Tucker's name she cringed. And she knew that Alec was acting stranger and stranger about having sex. Something wasn't right.

Jessie lit a cigarette, took a few drags, then threw it on the floor and put it out with her shoe. Normally she wouldn't be so careless, but she was beside herself. She couldn't stay there in the apartment. She grabbed her purse and left the apartment.

She walked down the street quickly, her mind racing. Alec was probably headed over to that fucker's house right now. They'd probably be laughing at her all night long. She lit another cigarette. She didn't know where she was headed, she just kept walking and smoking.

Jessie didn't know how much time had passed, but she suddenly found herself at Club 69. She went in and sat down at the bar and lit another cigarette.

Kelly, the bartender, approached Jessie and set a cardboard coaster down in front of her. "Hey there pretty lady, where's your husband?"

"Oh, who the fuck knows," Jessie mumbled.

"Oh, I see," Kelly said surprised, "what can I get the lady to numb the pain?"

"Fuzzy navel."

Jessie stared at her hands and played with her lighter. She picked at the edge of the nail polish on her fingernails. Kelly set down the drink in front of Jessie and said, "That one's on me, sweetie. Next one I'll start you a tab." Kelly started to walk away, then came back and said, "I don't know what he did, but he's a good boy. Don't stay mad."

Jessie didn't answer, so Kelly left her to her drink and her fidgeting.

After a while, the lights in the bar dimmed and the music on the jukebox stopped. A little ways away from the bar some disco lights came on over a wooden dance floor. A disembodied voice said, "Evening gals, Lady D is in the house." Thumping techno music began to fill the bar.

Jessie finished her drink and ordered another. When she was nearly done with the second drink, she sensed someone sitting down next to her at the bar. She glanced at the person and flashed a forced smile, and then returned to her own world.

"Can I freshen that drink for you?" the stranger asked.

Jessie looked back at the stranger. She was a butch who looked to be in her late twenties or early thirties. She was dressed in black jeans and a black sleeveless shirt. She had tattoos down her arm. She was heavy set, but handsome, with a well-cropped haircut. She smelt like men's cologne. Jessie thought she had seen her around the bar, but didn't know who she was. "Sure," Jessie answered.

The stranger motioned to Kelly, "A Miller Lite in the bottle and whatever the lady is drinking." Kelly gave the butch the once over, said nothing, and left to retrieve the drinks.

The butch turned to Jessie and announced, "I'm Sawyer," and she extended her hand.

"Jessie," Jessie said as she put her hand out to shake Sawyer's hand.

Sawyer took Jessie's hand, turned it over, and gently kissed it rather than shaking. After she kissed it, she held on to it longer than was necessary, all the while making direct eye contact with Jessie.

Kelly returned with the drinks. She set them down purposely loudly, and the bottle of beer bubbled over from the impact. "Oops," Kelly said in a dry, flat tone. "That's five dollars."

Sawyer threw a five-dollar bill on the bar and didn't bother to add a tip. Kelly took the bill and walked away without further comment.

"Somebody's having a bad night," Sawyer said in a voice loud enough for both Jessie and Kelly to hear. Then Sawyer turned her complete focus back to Jessie.

"So, what's a beautiful woman like you doing in a place like this all by yourself?" Sawyer asked.

Jessie was no stranger to pick up lines. Normally she could fend off unwanted advances fairly skillfully. But she was confused and hurt about all of the changes in Alec and the fuzzy navels had worked their magic, so she found herself unnecessarily open with Sawyer.

"My girlfriend wants to be a man."

"Oh. That's a twist. And what do you want, sweetheart?"

"I want to be with a woman."

"Well, then, it seems as if you and your lady-man are at cross purposes."

"Yup."

Sawyer picked at the edge of the label on her beer bottle for a few moments while she let the import of their conversation settle in with Jessie. She sensed that Jessie was looking at her, so she turned towards her. They looked at each other intently for a moment.

Sawyer began again, "If you want to talk some more, we could go to my place where it's quieter."

Jessie paused a moment. She was drunk, but she was painfully aware of the situation and her options.

"Okay."

Sawyer got them a cab and it wasn't long before the two of them were in Sawyer's apartment. They were careful to be quiet going in so as not to wake Sawyer's roommates who had long ago gone to bed. They headed back to Sawyer's bedroom.

Jessie knew that drunken sex was never very good. Jessie felt numb from a combination of the alcohol and her own emotional distress. She found the escapade less enjoyable than it should have been, though Sawyer had obviously bedded her share of women. Jessie tried to blank out her mind and not think about the terrible transgression that she was undertaking, but she was only somewhat successful.

When it was over, Jessie got dressed quickly and went to leave. Sawyer encouraged Jessie to stay the night, but Jessie was filled with regret and self-loathing. She hoped that Sawyer had only wanted a one-night stand, because regardless of what redeeming qualities that Sawyer might have, Jessie hoped that she would never see Sawyer again. Jessie had hoped that having sex with Sawyer would make her feel better, but it only reinforced that she was heartbroken.

Chapter 29

Across town Alec had long ago gone to sleep at Tucker's place, though Tucker had spent the night on the town and didn't come home until the wee hours of the morning. Alec had let himself in with the key that Tucker had given him several months earlier. Tucker was surprised to find Alec on the couch when he got home, and the opening of the door woke Alec.

"Hey kid, what're you doing here?" Tucker asked in a weary tone.

Alec blinked hard and sat up. "Jessie kind of freaked out on me. I think that she's really upset about my transition. She accused you and I of having an affair."

Tucker jerked his head back in disbelief and raised his eyebrows. "Us? Having an affair? Like, with each other?"

"Yup. Pretty funny, huh?"

"Well, yes. And no. That sucks, kid."

They sat in silence for a few moments.

Finally, Tucker said, "I'm sorry, but I gotta go to sleep. Can we do this tomorrow?"

"Today's tomorrow."

"Yeah, whatever, I'm too beat to argue semantics. You're not gonna kill yourself before noon or anything, right?" Tucker said.

"No. I'll be okay. We can talk later."

"Great." Tucker walked over to Alec and motioned for him to stand up. He gave him a firm hug and pounded his strong hands on Alec's back. Then Tucker turned and shuffled off to the bedroom and closed the door.

As the morning took shape into the day there was plenty of reflection going on in the city of Chicago. Jessie and Alec both wondered what the next step was. It seemed that Alec's transition was a point of contention that they were both surprised to discover. And it was almost too raw, too sensitive for both parties to try and reach a compromise on. Alec had to face that he felt misunderstood by Jessie, and so, yes, he did spend most of his time with Tucker. And Jessie had to face that she wanted to date a woman and that she might not ever feel fulfilled in a sexual relationship with Alec, regardless of his gender.

In the early evening Alec headed back home reluctantly. He wasn't looking forward to talking to Jessie. When he got to the apartment, Jessie wasn't there. She had left a note for him though.

Dear Alec:

I don't know what to say. Everything is so screwed up. I know that you and Tucker aren't sleeping together, I just said that because I was mad. But it does hurt me that you guys spend so much time together. I feel like Tucker understands you in a way that I can't. I love you, but there are so many things between us that I wish were different.

I did something stupid last night and I feel like I have to tell you so that you have all the information you need to move forward. I slept with someone I didn't know last night. I feel terrible about it, but if things were okay with us, I know that I never would have done it.

If you want to talk about all of this, please let me know. I'll understand if you hate me and don't want to talk at all, though.

Alec was floored. He couldn't believe what he was reading. He also couldn't decide whether to be infuriated or heartbroken. He didn't know what to feel or do. So he did the only thing that he could do, he grabbed a duffel bag from the closet and started emptying all of his clothes into it.

Chapter 30

Alec was sick of being misunderstood. He was relieved to move into Tucker's spare room. Tucker certainly wasn't the type of person who was given to deep emotional discussions, but something about his quiet masculinity reassured Alec. Alec knew that just the fact that Tucker would share his living quarters spoke volumes about how much he cared for Alec.

Alec didn't call Jessie and Jessie didn't call Alec. Alec was hurt by the betrayal, but more than that, Alec was hurt that Jessie didn't seem to understand him as a man.

Tucker and Alec settled into the bachelor pad life together. It was amusing to Alec that while he was shaving at the guest bathroom sink he knew that Tucker was doing the same in the master bath. No more fighting for space at the sink while Jessie tried to put on her makeup. Two vials of T, two stashes of syringes. Tucker walked around the house shirtless with boxer shorts on and Alec admired how nearly invisible the scars on his chest were, yearning deeply for the time when he too could do the same and hoping that his results would be as good. Sorting laundry began to require looking at underwear sizes as two sets of men's shorts and tops were in the mix rather than just one. Transition in Tucker's house was the rule rather than the freakish exception.

With Alec around, Tucker didn't seem to want to go out to the bars as often. Alec wondered if pleasant nights at home watching movies, or evening bike rides together were better than picking up strange women in bars and getting trashed. Tucker would often joke about their increasingly domestic lifestyle together, but when he brought it up, he didn't seem to mind.

One day on the worksite, Alec's cell phone rang, something that almost never happened during the day. Intently curious as to who would be calling in the middle of the day, he stopped his work and took the call, wondering if something was up with his supplier. He glanced down at the screen and saw, to his shock, "Smitty_Gail."

"Hello?"

"Alec baby, this is Gail."

"Hey, how are you? I haven't talked to you in forever."

"I know, baby. Listen, there's no good way to tell you this. Smitty's in the hospital, she's had a heart attack."

"Jesus. Is she okay?"

"Well, she's going into surgery for a bypass."

"Are you okay?"

"I've been better. Honey, I know that we haven't been there for you in a long while, but I wonder if you wouldn't come down to the hospital and sit with me a bit."

"Sure, yeah, definitely." Alec got the details about the hospital and hung up the phone. *Holy shit.* He could feel his heart pounding in his chest and his adrenaline pumping. He finished up what he was doing and went and found the site supervisor. He explained the situation and the supervisor told him to take the rest of the day off.

It had been over a year since Alec had seen Smitty or Gail. He missed them both desperately, but his friendship with Tucker had sort of filled the gap. Still, Tucker was his buddy, his brother. Smitty and Gail felt like his adopted parents. Admittedly, Alec was used to being without parents, but to suddenly find two people to fill that gap and to just as suddenly lose them, especially over his transition, had been a hard pill to swallow. It seemed like, for every good thing that his transition brought to him, there had to be some sort of equally bad thing to balance it out. It sucked.

Alec arrived at the hospital and found Gail in the waiting room on the floor where they performed the cardiac surgeries. Gail looked up from her knitting as Alec walked over to her chair. She got up and met Alec halfway across the room and gave him the hug of his life.

"Thanks for coming so quickly, baby," Gail said as she finally released Alec from her loving grip.

"No problem. How is she?"

"She's in surgery. It will take a long time. It's always a risky procedure, heart bypass surgery, I mean, they stop your heart. But she's got great doctors. I know that they will do their best."

The gravity of the situation settled in with Alec. "What can I do?"

"Just sit with me. Catch me up on your life and help distract me from worrying." Gail put her hands on each of Alec's arms and held him away from her to take a good look at him. "My goodness you've grown into a handsome man."

Alec recounted the last year of his life for Gail. Gail practically cheered when she learned about Alec meeting Tucker and about how well Alec's hormone therapy was going. She was loving and supportive when she heard that Alec and Jessie were separated. Alec realized that Gail was not so rigid in her ideas about sexuality and gender as Smitty was. Having lived so much of her life as a heterosexual, Gail seemed to feel that she hardly had any room to cast stones or to hold people to certain standards. Gail explained to Alec that she liked butch-femme culture, but most of all she liked Smitty. She had spent enough of her life unhappy that she wanted only the best for those that she cared about. If being a man made Alec happy, she wanted that for him. But given the choice between supporting Smitty and supporting Alec, she had to support Smitty. She hadn't wanted to abandon Alec in his hour of need, but it seemed that Smitty could not be convinced of Alec's legitimate need to transition.

Alec stayed with Gail throughout the surgery, taking little trips to the hospital cafeteria to get Gail coffee occasionally. After what seemed like an eternity, a doctor came out to the waiting room and approached Alec and Gail.

"You're here for Laura Smith?" the doctor asked.

"Yes?" Gail answered expectantly as she grabbed for Alec's hand and squeezed tight.

"The surgery went well. She'll have a long recovery ahead and there's never any promises with heart surgery, or any surgical recovery for that matter. But I think that things went as well as could be expected. She'll need to go into the surgical recovery room. You won't be able to see her for another hour or so. They'll probably keep her in ICU for a few hours after that and you ought to be able to see her then. And after that, if all goes well, she'll be transferred to a private room."

Gail closed her eyes tight and smiled with closed lips that seemed to border on a crying expression.

Alec stepped in. "Thank you, doctor. Will Gail and I be able to spend the night with her when she gets transferred to a private room?"

"Are you her son?"

Alec swelled with pride and confusion. "Uh…"

Gail broke in "Yes. I'm the medical representative and Alec is her son."

"Great. Well, you'll have to talk to the nurse on duty, but we can usually arrange for immediate family to stay overnight in the room."

"Thank you, doctor," Gail said. Gail smiled at Alec and gave him another monster hug.

Later that day Gail went to see Smitty when she woke up. Alec wasn't sure what to do. Alec thought that Smitty probably didn't want to see him. It was obvious that Gail needed Alec's support, though, so that she could be strong for Smitty. Later, while they were waiting for Smitty to be transferred to a private room, Alec broached the subject with Gail.

"Gail, I'm happy to be here. But I'm not sure that Smitty will want to see me, so what should I do?"

Gail sighed heavily and smiled at Alec. "Honey, Smitty loves you so much. You scared her and confused her with the gender stuff. She didn't understand it. By the time that she realized how bull-headed that she was being, it was too late. She couldn't overcome her pride to apologize to you. I know that she misses you though. I know that she regrets that she wasn't there for you when you needed her."

Alec was quiet.

"This heart attack is a big wake up call for all of us," Gail said. Alec noticed that Gail was trembling ever so slightly. She turned and looked Alec directly in the eye. "As soon as it happened, you were the first person that I thought of. That says a lot. When everything gets stripped away and the only thing that guides you is your heart, you make the choices that you should make. I wanted you to be here. I knew that Smitty would want you to be here too. I told her that you were here and how wonderful you were being. She was so happy that you were here to take care of me. It's harder for her to know that I have to go through this without her being able to help me through it than it is even for her to go through it herself. She trusts you. She loves you. She knows that you will take care of me."

Alec felt honored. Tucker was teaching Alec how to be a man on the outside, but honestly, Smitty had always been the best parts of what a good man was on the *inside*. Alec respected Smitty and her standards. He had been sad that he couldn't meet Smitty's standards in the past. To know that Smitty trusted Alec with her most precious thing, with Gail, it meant so much.

Chapter 31

After Smitty settled into a private room, Alec went to go see her. She had lots of tubes and machines hooked up to her and Alec hardly recognized her. She looked pale and exhausted, almost gaunt. As Alec entered the hospital room Smitty had her eyes closed, but when she sensed someone in the room she opened them.

"Hi, you," Smitty said in a small voice that seemed uncharacteristic coming out of such a large woman's body.

"Hi," Alec replied.

They sat together for a long while in uncomfortable silence. After a while, Smitty reached out for Alec's hand and he gave it to her. Alec looked at Smitty's face and saw that her eyes were welling up with tears. He squeezed her hand.

"Are you okay? Is something wrong? Should I call a nurse?" Alec asked, concerned.

Smitty shook her head no and choked back the tears so that they wouldn't flow. She took a few moments to compose herself.

"I was wrong," she said simply.

Alec wasn't entirely sure if he understood Smitty correctly, but he was fairly certain that Smitty was apologizing the best that she could for her poor reaction to Alec's transition.

"It's okay," Alec said.

"No, it's not. I abandoned you. That's a terrible thing to do. You should never talk to me again, but here you are. Thank you for taking care of Gail." Smitty paused, and then she looked Alec straight in the eye. "You're a good man."

Alec smiled sheepishly and squeezed Smitty's hand. "It's all good. We're good. Don't worry about any of that right now, you just concentrate on getting better, okay?"

Smitty's heart attack had been severe, and though the surgery went well, there had been some complications. In particular, Smitty's kidneys were not functioning correctly and the doctors were afraid that she might go into renal failure. The doctors kept Smitty longer than usual, a few weeks, doing supportive care and testing.

Alec and Gail took turns spending time with Smitty and tending to a never-ending parade of well-wishing visitors. Alec continued to work as much as possible, but he rarely made it back to Tucker's place and spent most nights at the hospital.

"So when do I get to meet your friend Tucker?" Gail asked one day when Alec came by to take his shift at the hospital.

"I don't think that he feels comfortable stopping by the hospital since he doesn't know you or Smitty," Alec answered.

"But he knows you, sugar," Gail offered with a tinge of confusion in her voice.

It was true that Tucker had seemed particularly apathetic about Smitty being in the hospital, but Alec hadn't had time to think about it much. "Yeah, I don't know, Tucker's just a hard guy to explain sometimes."

As Smitty slowly regained her strength, she and Alec began to talk more and play cards together during Alec's visits. One day Smitty swallowed more of her pride and broached the transgender topic with Alec.

"So, how are things going with your transition?"

Alec was surprised. "Fine. Are you sure that you wanna talk about that?"

"I know that I screwed it up the first time, but yeah, I care about you and I wanna know how you are."

"Well, the testosterone seems to be working well. I'm getting the results that I was hoping for and not having much in the way of negative side effects."

"That's quite a beard you have going there," Smitty noted, making Alec blush. "Are you happy?"

"Well, I feel better about myself, that's for sure. And work is going good. Things are kind of screwed up with Jessie right now, though, so I can't say that I'm totally happy right now."

"Gail told me that the two of you are separated."

The two of them sat in a reverent silence for a few moments. Since Smitty got sick Alec had been able to put the Jessie issue out of his mind, but all of the feelings began to wash back over him now: fear, anger, sadness, and frustration.

Smitty began to speak again. "You can take or leave what I have to say because, lord knows that I'm the last person you should listen to on the issue, but I think that you have to be true to yourself. And if that means that you have to transition to being a man and, god forbid, leave the butch-femme community, then that's what's gotta happen."

Alec was surprised, but relieved, to hear these words from Smitty.

Smitty continued. "Sometimes love isn't enough, ya know? Relationships are tough. Sometimes two people just aren't right for each other. And you can't push a square peg into a round hole without just making everyone uncomfortable and unhappy. You have to do your best to take a good hard look at what you and Jessie have and to do the right thing for both of you."

Alec knew that Smitty was right, but he was afraid. "What if there's nobody out there for me? What if no one wants to be with some transgender freakshow?"

"Now look here, son, I don't want to hear any crap like that from you. You are a good person. You have a good heart. You're a hard worker and you're smart as a whip. You got dealt a totally shitty hand in life and you turned it around all on your own. That's honorable. That's a sign of strong character." A moment later she added, "And I'm not exactly the best authority on the topic, but I'd say that you're a damn good looking guy."

Alec laughed, "Thanks." Smitty's words echoed in Alec's head, especially the word "son."

"I'm sure that there is a special lady out there for you. You just have to put yourself out there and take a chance."

Alec knew that Smitty was right about Jessie. He was mad that Jessie had cheated on him, but that wasn't the core of the problem in their relationship, it was just a symptom. Alec wasn't convinced that there really was someone out there for him, but he knew that staying with Jessie wasn't the answer either. For both of their sakes, it was time to put their relationship to rest. Alec hoped, though, that he wouldn't lose Jessie's friendship in the process.

Gail showed up to spend the night at the hospital and Alec went back to Tucker's place to go to bed. He had a hard time getting to sleep thinking about how it really was over between he and Jessie, or at least that it needed to be. Even though he was sad about this, he couldn't help but be happy that Smitty finally seemed to understand and accept him as a man.

A little before 5am Alec's cell phone rang, waking him up an hour earlier than usual. He was exhausted, but he got up and answered the phone.

"Hello?"

"Alec, it's Gail." Gail's voice seemed small and weak. "Alec, Smitty died."

Alec began to put the string of words together to make sense of them in his still sleepy state. "What?"

"Smitty's dead."

"Wha-what are you talking about? What happened?"

"She had another heart attack early this morning and went into cardiac arrest and they couldn't save her," Gail said in a flat voice.

"Jesus Christ. Where are you?"

"I'm home. I took a cab home."

"Are you okay? Do you want me to come over?" Alec asked.

"No. No, that's okay. I just wanted you to know," Gail answered. "I gotta go."

Before Alec could say anything more, Gail had hung up. He laid back down in bed and stared at the ceiling and felt more helpless than he ever had in his entire life.

Chapter 32

Alec had never known anyone who had died before and he had never been to a funeral. He didn't know what to expect. But the entire process of putting someone to rest seemed strange.

Alec thought that death was all about crying and grieving, but it turns out that there is so much to attend to in the days after a death, that one slips into a kind of "getting things done" mode. There are arrangements to be made and people to be notified. Alec stayed by Gail's side through all of this, and neither of them talked about Smitty or showed any outward sign of sadness.

The evening before the funeral there was a viewing at the funeral home. Alec wasn't sure that he wanted to go. The whole idea of a viewing seemed creepy, but Gail insisted that Alec come to help her get through the evening. So Alec put on his best suit and tie, packed his pockets with cotton handkerchiefs, and met Gail at the house to drive her over to the funeral home. Alec didn't drive very often, in fact he had only gotten a driver's license in order to have ID, but Gail was so used to Smitty driving all the time that Alec wanted to help ease that transition.

They were quiet in the car on the drive to the viewing. When they arrived at the funeral home, the director led Alec and Gail into the main gathering hall. The room was darkened, lit with dimmed side lighting and candles. There were chairs to the left and right of a center aisle which led down a long hall-like room. At the end of the room there was a casket with decorative flower arrangements on either side and behind it. The casket was closed.

The funeral director brought Gail, with Alec walking beside her with their arms interlaced, to the end of the room where the casket was located.

"Are you ready?" he asked Gail. Gail nodded her head yes. She squeezed Alec's hand and then let go of Alec's arm and walked towards the casket with the funeral director.

The director opened the casket. He turned, placed a hand gently on Gail's shoulder for a moment, and then retreated to the side of the room. As he did so he nodded kindly in Alec's direction.

Gail stood at the coffin for a long time with her back to Alec. Alec looked down at his feet. He didn't really want to see Smitty.

After a long time, other people began to arrive. Gail sat in a chair on the left hand side of the room. People would file into the hall, pass by the casket and pause, and then file on past Gail. They would stop and say a few words to Gail, sometimes crying, sometimes not. Gail was gracious and calm through the entire process. She almost seemed to be comforting others more than they were comforting her.

Alec wandered around the edges of the event. He helped direct people where to go and thanked them for coming. He told people where to send flowers or donations to the carpentry school for scholarships. Occasionally he would stop back by Gail and put a hand on her shoulder and she would silently put her hand over his.

Towards the end of the evening, when the viewing was officially over, Gail and the funeral director disappeared together into a side office to discuss the particulars of the next day's events. Alec was left alone in the hall with the open coffin. He paced nervously for a few moments, and then gave in.

Alec walked up to the coffin and peered into it. Smitty was dressed in the suit that Gail had eventually bought her for the wedding last year. The suit that Alec was supposed to have helped pick out on the day that he had "come out" to Smitty as a transsexual. She looked oddly unnatural. Perhaps, Alec thought, it was because she had more makeup on than she had ever worn in life. Looking at her lying there, it seemed very unreal.

After a moment or two, Alec went out to the parking lot for some fresh air. He took a cigarette out of his coat pocket and searched for matches and realized that, not normally being a smoker, he hadn't thought to bring any.

Suddenly, he felt light-headed and sat down exactly where he stood in the parking lot. He was shocked to find that he was suddenly weeping, something that he hadn't done since before he had started testosterone. The only thought in his head was the repeating word "why."

After a few moments, Gail emerged from the funeral home. Alec didn't want her to see him crying, but when she came up behind him he couldn't help but stand up and throw his arms around her and cry some more. Gail squeezed him tight to her and whispered, "It's okay, honey, let it out. She loved you so very much. She was so happy to talk to you those last few days. It's all fine between you now."

The day of the funeral, there was a mass at the church that Smitty and Gail attended. They may have been big lesbians, but Smitty and Gail were also devout Catholics who went to church every Sunday. They were valued members of their congregation. The church filled with other members of the congregation, hundreds of Smitty's students, piles of carpenters from the community, and their friends and neighbors. In one of the largest Catholic churches in northern Chicago, it was standing room only.

Alec had no idea that Smitty had touched so many other lives. Smitty and Gail had always made Alec feel so special, that he thought he was the only person they had ever opened their home and hearts to. But it turned out that Smitty and Gail were generous to everyone that they met, and in turn, there were many, many people who loved them and owed respects to Smitty.

After the mass and the long cycle of standing, kneeling, and sitting was over, Alec took his place as a pallbearer amongst six burly women and three other men. There was a procession of cars from the church to the burial site. The long line of mourners with orange flags on their cars created a traffic backup worse than the Edens Expressway at 5pm on a Friday night.

When they arrived at the cemetery it took a long time for everyone to find parking and get to the gravesite. At the grave there were white folding chairs for only about half of the people who arrived and a large popup tent over the casket and all of the flowers.

Alec rode with Gail to the funeral, and so was one of the first to arrive. He again helped carry the casket, and then settled back and watched the people slowly file in for the burial ceremony.

He noted, amongst the crowd, Jessie. It was the first time that he had seen her in maybe three months. He didn't even realize that Jessie knew that

Smitty had died. Alec was really glad to see Jessie.

The day was growing long and Alec was exhausted from so much interaction with so many people who were so upset. His feet were hurting in his dress shoes. He wasn't used to dressing this fancy. But he didn't let on to Gail. He owed it to Smitty to take care of Gail.

The mourners listened to nice things about Smitty, and then they all filed past to pay their last respects and to lay a rose on the closed casket. Gail and the pallbearers stood off to the side of the procession and received people as they filed past. Jessie came up to the casket and lay a yellow rose on it. She walked up to Gail and gave her a long hug. And then she walked up to Alec. She stood in front of Alec for a long time just looking into his eyes. She held her hands in front of her and Alec reached out for them. They held hands for a moment, and then they embraced.

Alec stayed until the bitter end of the ceremony, since Gail wanted to properly thank everyone who came. He saw Jessie start to head off to leave and he ran over to catch her.

"Hey Jessie," he said and she turned around to face him. "Thanks so much for coming."

"Of course" she said. "Is there anything that I can do?"

Alec was completely spent from the last few days' events, and from the weeks leading up to Smitty's death. He didn't have any strength left and he wasn't able to stop himself from saying, "Would it be all right if I came home for awhile?"

Jessie smiled uncertainly. "I would love for you to come home, if you don't hate me too much," Jessie said.

Alec didn't know what to say. Too many things had happened in too short of a time. "I don't hate you. I need you right now."

Chapter 33

The days and weeks after Smitty died were some of the strangest of Alec's life. If Smitty had been Alec's mother, it would be well accepted by society that Alec would have a long and painful grieving process. But because Smitty was just Alec's "friend," there was an eerie sense of the world continuing to turn just as it always had.

For Alec, the world was suddenly divided up into "us" and "them." "Us" were those who knew and loved Smitty the best: Alec, Jessie, and, of course, Gail. "Them" was everybody else. "They" didn't understand. "They" didn't care. If Alec couldn't ever see or talk to Smitty again, he felt like all that he wanted to do was be with Jessie and Gail.

During Smitty's last days Tucker had mostly left Alec alone. Since Tucker had never known Smitty, it didn't seem so strange that he didn't visit Smitty in the hospital or attend the funeral. Tucker's absence at these events, though likely not meant as malicious, drove a sort of wedge between Alec and Tucker. Alec was in the "us" part of the world and Tucker, for only situational reasons, was in the "them" part of the world.

Alec moved back in with Jessie and they consoled each other through the weeks immediately following Smitty's death. They were kind to each other, and affectionate but not sexual. They made sure to resume their Sunday night dinners with Gail. They bonded in their grief.

Eventually, the time came to rejoin the world. Gail was determined to honor Smitty's memory by continuing to operate the carpentry school. Smitty had many, many loving alums who offered to pitch in and help with the school. Gail assembled a pool of instructors who alternated teaching so that the school could go on, while allowing the women who taught to continue working outside of the school.

Life went on for Alec and Jessie, too. Alec was fairly certain that neither of them had any illusions about a reconciliation and that they both knew that they were together for the moment only because they needed each other. One night a few months after the funeral, they finally sat down and had a long talk.

"Jessie, you are one of the most important people in my life and I love you," Alec began, "but there are some things that I need to know, that we need to get clear."

"I know," Jessie said.

"I need to be with someone who accepts me as a man, completely. I need to be with someone who wants to be with a man."

"Alec, I love you so much. But you're right. I want to be with a woman. When you decided to transition, I thought that I could handle it. I thought that I loved you enough. But the truth is that, when I think about you losing your female body, it makes me very sad. I want to be with someone who has a woman's body. In fact, I don't even want to be with a stone butch. I want to be with someone who can share their body with me. I want to have that part of a sexual relationship."

Alec nodded in understanding.

Jessie continued, "I think masculine, butch women are SO sexy, but the reason that I think that they are sexy is because, underneath, they are really women. That's what I like. I'm so sorry that I didn't figure that out before I hurt you."

"It's okay," Alec answered. "It's not like you signed up for all of this at the beginning."

They both paused. "Is it okay if we stay friends, though?" Alec said.

Jessie started to tear up a bit. "Definitely, if you'll still have me as a friend," Jessie answered.

"Yes, of course."

They hugged each other tightly and Jessie gave Alec a small kiss on the lips.

"I can start looking for a new place soon," Alec said after they finished their embrace.

"Well, are you gonna be able to afford that? Weren't you going to have your chest surgery soon?"

"Yeah, but I can push that back. Anyway, recovery would suck to do on my own right now."

Jessie thought for a second. "You know, if you wanted to stay here until after you recovered from your surgery, that would be okay with me."

"Really?" Alec was shocked.

"Yeah, I mean, I can't afford to live on my own either. And I can't bear the thought of you either having to put off your surgery or having to recover alone. And besides, we've been living here together for a few months now with no hanky panky and I feel pretty okay about it, what about you?"

"It's been great staying here. But are you sure? I mean, I'm gonna be out of commission for a while, and I'm gonna need a lot of help. Do you really want to take on that responsibility if we're not even dating?"

"You're my friend. Friends help friends. It's the least I can do after I cheated on you."

Chapter 34

Alec had been researching surgeons for his chest surgery since the beginning of his transition. He'd also been saving money for the surgery all that time.

With Dr. Taffe's help, Alec was able to find a doctor in the Chicago area who was willing to evaluate Alec in a way that would allow his hysterectomy to be covered by his health insurance. When he thought he would have to pay out of his pocket for the hysterectomy, he had debated whether he even wanted a hysterectomy for a long time.

His primary concern was getting rid of his breasts. They made him uncomfortable. His second biggest priority was improving the size and function of his penis (formerly his clitoris), which testosterone had improved greatly, but there was still more improvement that could be made. Work on his penis would have to wait for him to save more money, though, because he wanted to be sure to get that surgery done by the best doctor available.

He felt that his internal reproductive organs were really unnecessary, really just breeding grounds for cancer, though they didn't trouble him particularly. Also, getting rid of his reproductive organs assured that, even if he had to go off of testosterone some day for health reasons, that he'd never get another period. When he found out insurance could cover the procedure, he decided to go for it.

Insurance would not cover his top surgery though. He wanted the best results possible, with as little scarring as possible. He had seen some pretty horrible chest surgery results, and he didn't want to end up like that. He also knew that a bad chest surgery might mean more revision surgeries in the future, which he wanted to try and avoid. He investigated surgeons all over the country, and even some in Canada, but decided that it would be better to stay in the Chicago area so that he could get the hysterectomy and the top surgery done near the same time in order to minimize the amount of time that he would be out of work recovering. He found a doctor in Wilmette, Illinois, which was very close to Chicago, who had experience with FTM top surgeries and seemed to do reasonably good work.

Alec had been on T for about a year and a half. The hormones had made their own amount of impressive change in Alec's chest. The hormones, along with doing physical labor every day, had built up the muscles in his chest. Binding his breasts daily for nearly three years had also done its own kind of magic. Squashing one's breast tissue every day breaks down the tissue and ends up making the breasts flatter and saggier, not an ideal outcome for the average person, but ideal for someone who'd rather not have breasts at all.

The plan was for Alec to have a vaginal hysterectomy first so as to avoid unsightly scarring. The surgeon would leave the ovaries since they would assist with Alec's natural production of testosterone. He would have his hysterectomy in Chicago and if all went well with that surgery, go to

Wilmette two weeks later and have his top surgery. Then Alec would take a full 8 weeks off of work to recover.

Jessie drove Alec to the hospital for his hysterectomy. The prep work and the surgery went well and Alec spent two days in the hospital recovering. Then he went home to await his top surgery date and to hope for good health in the interim. Jessie cooked for Alec and helped him with whatever he needed when she wasn't at work.

Alec had plenty of time on his hands during the two weeks, since he was determined not to overdo things and jeopardize his top surgery. He tried to call Tucker repeatedly, to no avail, thinking that now was a perfect time to catch up on any movies that he had missed lately. Plus, Alec was nervous about his top surgery, and he wanted to commiserate with Tucker, who had already gone through the procedure several years earlier. Tucker had already missed Alec's hysterectomy, and Alec didn't want him to miss his top surgery too.

Alec had a sense that Tucker was mad at him and was avoiding him. Alec knew that Tucker wasn't used to having close friends, and Alec wondered if Tucker was somehow jealous of the time that Alec had been spending with Gail and Jessie over the last many months since Smitty had gotten sick.

The two weeks between surgeries seemed to take a long time to pass, but Alec was healthy enough at the end of them to move forward with his top surgery. Jessie drove Alec to Wilmette late one afternoon and they stayed in a hotel there overnight. The surgery was in the morning the next day, and by evening they were coming back to the hotel post-op.

Alec slept for the rest of that first day. The next day they returned to Chicago and Alec slept most of that day too. Jessie helped him change his bandages and empty the drains that he had in his chest. The drains were awkward and uncomfortable. After a few days Alec was able to go back to the doctor in Wilmette and get the drains taken out, which was one of the most uncomfortable parts of the entire procedure. After the drains were out, though, Alec felt 100% better physically.

Emotionally, Alec was on a bit of a roller coaster. A lot had happened in a relatively short period of time. His body was completely different now, and nearly unrecognizable. When he looked in the mirror he felt like he was looking at someone else. Not only had everything changed, but he was a long way from looking the way that he would once everything had healed. He was severely bruised and had bandages sewn to his nipples to protect them. He looked a little like he had been beaten or like he was some sort of Frankenstein experiment. It was hard to see past those things and to be optimistic about what he would look like when he had healed. The sudden change was a difficult thing to comprehend, but Alec was happy and grateful to Jessie for her support. He felt more emotional than he had since Smitty had died.

Slowly, Alec began to recover more and more. About two weeks after his top surgery, he went in to get the dressings on his nipples removed. The dressings were very uncomfortable and made washing and sleeping difficult. When the dressings came off Alec was surprised at how his nipples looked. They were peeling a bit and it seemed that there was a bit of dead tissue. They looked like they had seen better days, but the doctor seemed to think that they were healing satisfactorily. *Easy for him to say, he's not the one with weird looking nipples!*

After the initial period of discomfort, Alec was happy with the progress of his recovery from both surgeries. It was still too early to be able to tell how much sensation he would regain in his chest and nipples, or to tell how lightly his scars would heal. He couldn't be as active as he wanted, but he consoled himself by remembering that he needed to take it easy so that he could get back to work at the end of the eight weeks and so that his scars would heal as well and as lightly as possible. A setback in recovery would mean more time off of work, and he couldn't afford that financially or mentally. Or worse, he might damage his healing chest and it might end up looking bad or needing more expensive surgery.

Alec took the free time that he had to think about what he wanted to do with his career and to study on the internet towards more carpentry certification. He also took a cue from his transmen brothers and documented his transition on a website that he created during his recovery. He splurged and got a digital camera and painstakingly took photos of his body as it progressed through recovery.

He also began to wonder if he hadn't been unfairly harsh on the Chicago FTM group members. He came to realize that the real reason that they had made him uncomfortable was that they highlighted his own fears and insecurities. They represented the concrete possibility of transition, which had scared Alec more at the time than he had realized. They also made him realize how unsure of himself as a man that he was. Finally, because most of them were from different educational and class backgrounds than Alec, they made him feel defensive about his history and his credentials. Knowing and being accepted by Tucker and Jessie had proven to Alec that he could hold his own amongst college educated people from middle class families. He learned that he was just as smart, capable, and valuable a person as people who came from different backgrounds. Alec realized that the group wasn't the problem, that it was his own feelings about himself that was the problem. He decided to reach out again to the group and to begin doing things with them socially.

Returning to the group post-op and with plenty of T behind him also made him feel like he had more "street cred." He was now in a position to help others as well as to make friends. On his return to the group, he found the majority of them to be decent people worth knowing. It gave him one more circle of understanding and accepting friends with whom he could relax completely.

Chapter 35

T ucker had let his emotions go out on a limb when he befriended Alec. And he had come to enjoy living with Alec in spite of himself. When Smitty had gotten sick, Alec had basically disappeared from Tucker's life all of the sudden. Tucker could understand that at first, but he didn't get why the situation persisted even after Smitty died. Tucker didn't like being vulnerable, and Alec had put him in a vulnerable position. Tucker felt used, like Alec only came around when he needed something from Tucker. So when Alec started calling again, Tucker blew him off.

Tucker spent the better part of the evening surfing the internet and drinking at home. It had been a while since he had made the transguy web rounds. He had a selection of official sites like *The Transitional Male* and *FTM International* bookmarked, along with a large selection of personal blogs. Eventually he made his way to the porn sites. These weren't commercial porn about freakish "she-males," this was homegrown porn, pictures and stories from real FTMs posted for other FTMs and their SOFFAs (Significant Others, Friends, Family, and Allies).

Tucker had never been much for porn. He didn't read erotica and he didn't look at nudie pictures. Most of it was garbage anyway. Tonight the pictures of the FTMs oddly fascinated him, though. Their muscles firm under tattoos. And that same piercing look in all of their eyes. Sad, but determined eyes.

After about an hour of looking at the pictures, Tucker felt a yearning that had been building inside needed to be attended to. He left his seat at the computer and went and lay down on the couch. He kept an image in his mind of one of the more attractive and well-built FTMs from the website. He imagined the man going down on him and sucking his cock. In his mind, though, Tucker's cock wasn't the two-inch-when-erect penis that he had in real life, but instead it was long and full. The stranger sucked him until he ejaculated in the transman's mouth. The juice ran down the man's face and neck and mingled with his chest hair across the scars on his chest. The man turned over Tucker and began fucking him in the ass with his own hard cock. Tucker moaned in ecstasy as the stranger pressed over and over again against Tucker's imaginary prostate gland. The man rocked inside of Tucker harder and harder, faster and faster. Then, the man took off his condom and put his dick into Tucker's vagina.

The image was pure fantasy, but the concept pressed at the edges of Tucker's comfort zone. The idea of anal penetrative sex kept Tucker's sense of manhood intact, though it had gay overtones. Adding the vaginal intercourse was exciting in that it was dangerous ground for Tucker's sense of self. Tucker was intensely excited by the idea of being penetrated vaginally, but he was terrified of ever having it happen in real life.

Tucker's fantasy continued as the transman began to fuck Tucker hard into his cunt until they both came. Tucker rolled over and took the man into his arms and brought the gorgeous stranger's face up to his own to kiss him. Much to Tucker's surprise, when he pulled the man's face up to his own, he found that he was looking into his old college friend Doug's eyes.

Tucker shuddered with a start. He had his eyes closed during the fantasy while he masturbated, but the sudden image of Doug in his mind forced him to open his eyes fast, as if waking up from a nightmare.

Tucker's buzz had nearly worn off anyway, but now he was conscious of being painfully sober. He got up and went to the kitchen counter where he had left the bottle of Shakers Vodka. He didn't even bother getting his glass from the other room and instead took the cap off and took a long, hard swig directly from the bottle. Then he grabbed a new glass from the cabinet, filled it with ice, poured vodka over the ice, and squeezed some of the lime that was still sitting on the counter into the drink.

He took a few sips from the glass and stared straight ahead. He tried very hard not to think of anything at all. But it was no use, he couldn't get that image of Doug out of his mind. He took another sip. He felt a sudden mix of fear, sadness, confusion, and rage. His bottom lip quivered just ever so slightly. He picked his glass up off of the counter, turned to the sink, and smashed the glass against the stainless steel.

The next day it was hard for Tucker to get out of bed. He had a pretty vicious hangover. That hadn't happened in a long time. He dragged himself around the apartment getting ready for work. He contemplated calling in sick. He certainly had plenty of sick time saved up. Of course, what would he do if he stayed home all day? Think? Drink? The options didn't seem good. So he made his way to work.

At work he hid in his cubicle for most of the morning, slowly eating a single rice cake and drinking sparkling water to nurse his hangover. The one thing that greasy meaty food was really good for was kicking a hangover, this he remembered from his early college days. But the thought of eating meat, the thought of the smell of it, made Tucker feel like retching.

Around mid-afternoon Tucker began to feel more human again. The nausea was gone, but a faint headache was still hanging with him. His supervisor, Richard, appeared at the opening to his cubicle. "How are my numbers coming?"

Tucker blinked hard as Richard's words seemed to grate on the back side of his eyeballs. "I'm running a little behind today, Tucker said quietly.

"Behind? *BEHIND?* I need those today."

"Well, when you gave me the assignment at 7 o'clock last night, you failed to mention that little factoid," Tucker responded, trying not to get too mad. Mostly he didn't want to raise his voice too loud and irritate the pain behind his eyes.

"Look, I need it now."

"Well, that's just too damn bad, it'll take me at least a couple of more hours to finish running the model," Tucker responded, feeling his head start to pound again.

Richard paused a moment staring at Tucker, as if this would change the reality of the situation. Then he turned and huffed back to his office.

Tucker was fairly certain that Richard was just busting his balls. He probably didn't even need it today. Or, more likely, he hadn't bothered to figure out when he needed it, and then found out today that he had put it off way too long and was screwed. It was typical, Richard was always pulling shit like that and trying to blame it on Tucker.

One of Tucker's other coworkers, Jason, appeared in the cubicle next to Tucker after having been gone all day. "Where've you been?" Tucker asked.

Jason swung around the edge of his cubicle. "I went and met with the Hampshire account." Jason paused, seeming uncertain. "It went pretty well."

Tucker wondered if his hangover was affecting his hearing. "Did you say the Hampshire account?"

"Yeah, why?"

"I was supposed to work on that project."

Jason looked confused. "I don't know, dude. Richard asked me last week to go to this meeting. Honestly, I was kind of freaked out about it. I know it's an important account. I was sort of surprised that he gave it to me, actually." Jason paused. "I didn't know that you wanted it, dude, or I would have mentioned it to you."

"It's all right," Tucker told Jason. But it wasn't okay. It wasn't okay at all. Richard knew that the Hampshire account was a real opportunity to try out some new methods. And he also knew that Tucker had a better feel for that sort of thing than any actuary at the firm, certainly better than Jason, who was barely out of school. That asshole Richard had Tucker doing his lame ass grunt work while he gave away the projects that Tucker *should* be doing to beginners.

Tucker looked at his computer screen. He closed his eyes and felt the blood vessels pounding behind the lids. He took a quick glance around his cubicle. Then he got up, walked out the door of the office, went down the elevator to the garage, got in his car, and drove away.

Chapter 36

One afternoon at Trader Joe's Jessie was stocking Thai Kitchen dinner mixes when she heard someone behind her say her name softly. She turned around and after a split second of computation, recognized the face.

"Hey Nina, long time no see." Jessie put out her arms and gave Nina a warm hug. "How are you doing?"

"Oh, you know, still in school. I'm not sure that I'll ever finish this PhD. But I'm good, I can't complain really. My funding is still solid and I guess that's all a career student can really ask for. Of course, having a warm body to come home to would be nice too."

Jessie had met Nina a few years earlier in a lesbian book group that she belonged to briefly. The purpose of the book group, of course, had very little to do with reading. Mostly it was an excuse to get together and gossip and to scope out potential partners.

Nina was in her early thirties and was studying anthropology at the

University of Chicago. She had gotten her bachelor's degree in women's studies at Smith College in Massachusetts and had made the romantic rounds there as a femme lesbian. She wasn't a high femme by any means, though, more along the lines of an "LL Bean" femme. She liked to feel girly, but she wasn't above getting her hands dirty. She kept her nails trimmed short.

After Smith, Nina had gone on to get a master's degree in feminist theory at Minnesota State University. While getting her master's degree, a casual friend of hers, a gay man named James, was unexpectedly diagnosed with AIDS and quickly declined and died. Even though she wasn't close to James, he was the first person that she knew in her life who had died. He was also the first person that she had known with AIDS. The gay community at MNSU was tightly knit, and James' death affected everyone profoundly.

Nina finished her master's degree, but James' death made her reflect deeply on her own life, plans, and perceptions. She realized that anyone can die at any time, and this made her wonder if she was making the most of her life and doing all that she could to make the world a better place.

At age 27, rather than continuing on with her original plan of getting her PhD and teaching women's studies, Nina had taken time off of school. She had a sense that her worldview was unbalanced because of her studies. She began to wonder if she had fallen into the trap of rebelling so thoroughly against the gender inequality that she perceived in the world that she was reinforcing the paradigm in her own head by focusing too much on women's plight. She began to become disenchanted with feminism for feminism's sake. She began to worry that she was creating her own perverse stereotypes of gender in her mind.

She took a one-year internship at a nonprofit in Minnesota that provided services to disabled people. While there, she worked closely with one of the staff people, a man named Morgan. The two of them worked well together and hit it off. Morgan quickly fell for Nina and began to make romantic advances towards her.

Nina struggled for months with the idea of dating a man. She had identified her entire life as a lesbian and a feminist, and dating a man seemed anathema to all that she had learned and that she stood for. Eventually, the natural attraction between them overwhelmed Nina's misgivings though, and the two of them slept together. She learned more about men over that year than she had learned over the rest of her life.

Though Nina struggled with the decision to have that first sexual encounter with Morgan and with what that meant for her radical lesbian feminist identity, after the act, it didn't seem like as much of a big deal. Nina realized that a single physical act didn't change who she was inside or alter any of her experiences in life. Morgan was a gentle and loving man and their sexual relationship was satisfying to Nina.

Morgan was kind and smart, funny and generous. He also was old fashioned. He wanted a wife and kids and a white picket fence. He wanted to live out his days in rural Minnesota and grow old in a rocker on the front porch of an old farmhouse. Nina knew that wasn't the life for her. Nina enjoyed rural life in small doses, but she preferred living the vibrant life of a city. She enjoyed politics and philosophy. She thrived on interacting with other people who had different viewpoints. She didn't want to settle down far away from the hustle and bustle and interact primarily with one person.

Further, though being with Morgan opened her eyes to understanding men better and appreciating them more, Nina still didn't really consider herself straight, or even bisexual, really. She still identified as lesbian. Faced with the undeniable fact that she was capable of being attracted to and enjoying sex with a man made her begin to think deeply about her sexuality, though. She became more and more interested in the boxes that we all squeeze ourselves into and the labels that we apply. She wondered about the "queering" of boundaries.

It was clear to Nina that, though she cared about Morgan and enjoyed their time together, she couldn't be the straight housewife that Morgan was hoping for, and so, after her internship was over, she left Minnesota and a heartbroken Morgan, and returned to graduate school. But this time Nina had a new perspective and a broader focus on society and how gender roles develop.

Nina came to Chicago to work on her PhD in gender theory through the anthropology department at the University. She returned to dating women, but she also began to have an interest in the blurred lines of gender identity. She was fascinated with people who didn't fall neatly into society's gender roles, and her studies afforded her plenty of opportunity to seek out such folks. She found herself attracted more and more to genderqueers (people who didn't follow society's conventions for gender) and female to male transsexuals. She dated a few of them, but got burned badly by misogynist self-centered FTMs who were more concerned with their transitions than with loving Nina.

"So Jessie, what about you? Are you seeing anybody these days?"

"Well I was," Jessie said, suddenly remembering Nina's interest in gender identity. "It's kind of ironic, really. I was dating this great woman Alec and..."

Nina cocked her head and leaned in to encourage Jessie to continue.

"You're gonna think that I'm a terrible person."

"Oh, nonsense, what is it?"

"Alec is transitioning to being a man. I thought I could handle it, but I just couldn't. So we broke up."

"Oh. I'm so sorry, Jessie," Nina said with genuine empathy.

"Yeah. It's okay, though. We saved the friendship. In fact, he's my roommate now. He just recently recovered from some surgery, so he's been staying with me until he gets over it."

"Jessie, that's so caring of you to help him through such a difficult time."

"Well, I do love him. I just can't help being a big old dyke." Jessie smiled sheepishly.

Nina chuckled. "Well, it was really great to see you. Tell your friend that I wish him a fast recovery." Nina reached out and squeezed Jessie's arm and started to turn to leave.

Jessie suddenly put two and two together and called out to Nina. "Hey Nina, I don't suppose you'd like to come over to our place for dinner sometime, would you?"

Nina stopped and turned back to face Jessie. "You know, that would be really nice. Thank you." Nina dug in her purse and produced a business card and gave it to Jessie. "Kind of geeky of me to have cards, I know, but I interview so many people for school that it just got easier to print some cards up than keep having to write my information down. Give me a call or drop me an email and let me know when is good for you."

Jessie took Nina's card and said, "Great, I'll talk to you soon."

A week later Jessie called Nina and invited her over to dinner. Near the end of the conversation, Jessie laid her cards on the table.

"Nina, I'm so glad that you'll come to dinner and I'll be glad to catch up, but I must admit that I have an ulterior motive."

"Oh?" Nina said curiously.

"My roommate, Alec, he's a really nice guy and I want the best for him. I think that the two of you might hit it off."

Nina's tone turned skeptical. "Didn't you guys used to date? How would you feel about it if we DID hit it off?"

"I think that it would be fine. Alec and I haven't been romantic for a long time. I'm pretty much over it. We just weren't right for each other relationship wise. In fact, I regret now that I never thought to call you for advice on the whole thing."

"Hindsight is always 20/20," Nina reassured Jessie.

"And besides, if he's going to be with someone else, I'd rather it be with someone great like you than someone who's no good for him."

"That's really very sweet of you to say," Nina demurred. "I can tell that you care about him very much and I'm honored that you would trust me with someone who means so much to you. I'd love to come over to dinner and I'd love to meet Alec."

"Great! We'll see you soon."

Chapter 37

Alec was nearly 100% again. He had taken off as much time from work as possible to recover. Swinging hammers isn't exactly all that much fun after major abdominal surgery and having all the fat scraped off of your chest muscles. Alec's doctor had managed to get his insurance to pay for the hysterectomy by saying it was needed to alleviate menstrual cramps. This was, of course, a lie, since Alec hadn't had a period since not long after he had started hormones. But he had still had to pay for the mastectomy out of his own pocket, and then make ends meet without income for a few months. So it was important that Alec return to work as soon as possible.

Jessie was outstanding the entire time, providing tender loving care as well as meals and laundry. Alec didn't know how he could possibly repay her, but he hoped he'd have the opportunity by being friends for life with her.

In another week and a half Alec would start a new carpentry job. He started trying to do low-key exercise to get his muscles working well again, but he was still sore and his chest scars were still healing. He was pleased with the way that his scars were healing and he thought that eventually things would look pretty good.

The Friday night before Alec went back to work, Jessie made a big celebration dinner and told Alec that she was inviting an old friend over to have dinner with them. Alec was happy to be going back to work. In fact, he was happy just to be getting out of the apartment every day again, so he didn't make much of the announced dinner guest.

Friday night came and Jessie put out a great spread. She set the lighting just so with candles everywhere and the lamps on dim. She put on a Norah Jones CD. Alec was in the shower, so he didn't notice the mood setting activities. Nina knocked on the door right on time at seven o'clock, and Alec emerged from the bedroom tucking in his shirt. "I'll get the door, Jessie." He noticed that the lights were nearly out but didn't quite understand. "Why's it so dark in here?" he said as he headed to the front door and opened it.

There in the hallway was a vision so lovely that it took Alec's breath away: a woman with long brown hair and brilliant green eyes in a wispy spring dress and simple flat sandals. She was holding a small bouquet of flowers.

"Hi. I'm Nina. You must be Alec."

Alec missed a beat like a junior high school boy at his first school dance.

"Is it okay if I come in?"

Alec snapped back to reality. "Oh, of course, come on in," he said, flustered. "Jessie, Nina's here," he called out, and then turned to Nina.

Nina held out the bouquet to Alec. "These are for you. Jessie told me that you're just heading back to work after some surgery. I just wanted to wish you good health and good luck back on the job."

"Thanks." Alec was shocked. A woman had never given him flowers before, especially a beautiful stranger.

Jessie emerged from the kitchen. "Hey Nina, thanks for coming over" she said as she went over to give Nina a hug.

"Are you kidding? A free home cooked meal? How could a starving graduate student resist?"

Alec's heart sank a little. *A graduate student. Probably too smart for him.*

"Why don't you two sit down on the couch and I'll get some drinks? What will you have, Nina? We've got a pretty good selection."

"How about a vodka and cranberry juice?"

"Yup, no problem," Jessie said as she turned back towards the kitchen.

"Do you need any help, Jessie?" Alec asked.

"No, no. You just go keep Nina company," Jessie said with a wink.

Alec couldn't believe his eyes. This was a setup. His ex-girlfriend was setting him up with this gorgeous creature. *God bless you Saint Jessie.*

Alec sat down on the couch and turned on his rusty charm. It had been a while. In a few moments Jessie appeared with Nina's drink and a Miller Lite for Alec. It was the first beer that he had had since the surgery because of all of the pain killers that he was on for so long.

Alec wondered how much Jessie had told Nina about his situation. But it wasn't long before the regular questions led them to Nina's field of study, and then Alec breathed a sigh of relief. Nina was smart, no doubt about it, but she didn't talk over his head. She didn't talk down to him either.

She gently flirted with him throughout dinner and he returned the favor. She made him feel really sexy and good inside. She was just wonderful.

Around ten o'clock Jessie suddenly was overcome with exhaustion and implored Alec and Nina to feel free to stay up and continue to talk and not quit on her account. She hugged her goodbyes to Nina and Alec got up and walked Jessie back to the bedroom. He whispered to her, "You're a sneaky woman. You're a great woman, but a sneaky one." Jessie smiled broadly at him. "Thank you," he said and gave her a quick peck on the cheek and a gentle hug. He regretted that he was still sensitive to tight squeezes because he wanted to hug Jessie hard to his flat chest.

Nina and Alec stayed up and talked for a few more hours until it became obvious that Alec was fading. "You should get your rest so you'll be strong for work on Monday morning," Nina said.

"It's late, can I put you in a cab?" he asked.

"Sure, that would be nice," she answered.

Alec called the cab and then walked Nina down to the sidewalk and waited with her for the taxi to arrive.

"Would it be okay if we hung out together some time again?" Alec asked hopefully.

"That would be wonderful," Nina answered.

Just then, a taxi pulled up to the curb. Alec hugged Nina and noted that she seemed to know not to squeeze too hard. He leaned in the window of the cab and handed the cabbie a twenty and a ten-dollar bill. "Take the lady wherever she'd like and keep the change." He moved to the back of the cab and opened the door for Nina. She got in part of the way, then leaned out towards Alec and kissed him gently on the lips. Then she got in and Alec closed the door and watched the cab drive away.

Alec stood there looking after the car for a long time. He had a strange feeling and tried to place it. And then it suddenly occurred to him. He felt normal.

Chapter 38

Dating Nina came easily for Alec. Nina was the consummate femme, but she was also trans-savvy. Nina was a trans-*sensual*, something that Alec had read about on the internet, but didn't really believe existed. A transsensual finds themself attracted to transgender or transsexual persons.

With Nina, Alec felt like there were no expectations for what his gender should be or what should define him as a person. Nina told him that she considered gender a spectrum rather than a dichotomy. She thought that sex was between the legs, but gender was between the ears. And once something was between the ears, it could be as varied as the spectrum of human experience and feeling.

Alec didn't want to rush into a new relationship, shell shocked from the experience with Jessie, but Alec felt at ease with Nina right away. Nina was smart and kind, sexy and gentle. And Nina had this wonderful way of finding Alec's strengths and highlighting them. Being around Nina made Alec feel good about himself.

The two of them complemented each other so well that it was difficult, and seemingly unnecessary, to put off the inevitable. They fell in love quickly and completely.

At the start of the summer, Nina helped Jessie find a new roommate from amongst her classmates at the University, and then they carted the few things that Alec owned over to Nina's place a few miles west. Nina joined the Sunday night dinners at Gail's place and Jesse continued to come. The four of them became a sort of modern queer family. Before long Nina, Alec, and Gail were ganging up on Jessie and scheming to set up her up on blind dates with a parade of handsome young butches.

One evening Nina and Alec stopped by Club 69 on a Saturday night after going out to the movies together. Neither of them made it by the club very often anymore, so it was sort of a nice, fun end to a pleasant evening.

After the two of them had been there for about an hour, Nina noticed someone at the bar get up and stumble a bit on his way to the bathroom. "Whoa, that guy's had a little too much," Nina commented.

Alec looked up and noted the drunken man. There was something familiar about the person, but at first Alec the connection didn't register. Then, suddenly, his heart jumped in his chest. "Oh my god, that's Tucker." While Alec was accustomed to being around Tucker when he was drinking, he had never seen Tucker looking out of control like a classic drunk.

Alec had been trying to make contact with Tucker for months, since before he had even started dating Nina. He had been trying ever since Smitty's funeral in fact. Tucker had put Alec off for several months, and then just stopped returning his calls entirely.

Alec let Tucker go to the bathroom while he let his heart settle down from his throat. Nina was quiet. Alec watched Tucker return to the barstool and sit down again. And then he kissed Nina on the top of her head and got up from his seat and walked over to the bar.

"Hey stranger, long time no see," Alec said to Tucker as he slid into the barstool next to Tucker.

Tucker reeled around with an exaggerated turn of the head and looked at Alec blankly for an instant. Then a sudden recognition flashed across Tucker's cloudy hazel eyes. "Hey kid, what's the good word?" Tucker said without a hint of emotion in his voice.

"I, uh, I tried to call you for a while, but you didn't return my calls," Alec said.

"Yeah, well, I guess I was too busy."

"You don't look very busy now," Alec continued.

"Why don't you just fuck off and leave me alone?" Tucker replied with sudden anger. He stood up quickly, causing him to lose his balance, which only seemed to piss him off more. He reached into his wallet, grabbed a wad of bills and threw them on the bar, and stumbled out of the club.

Alec headed back to the table quickly. "I'm sorry babe. I gotta go after him."

Nina put her finger to her lips. "Shhh! Go, go!"

Alec rushed out into the warm summer night air and looked left and right for where Tucker had headed. He spotted him a half a block down the street and he ran after him, catching up with the drunken Tucker easily.

"Look, I don't know what I did to piss you off, but we need to talk," Alec said in a raised tone as he caught up to Tucker.

"I don't need to say anything. Seems like you've got plenty of other people to talk to, so why don't you go talk to them."

"What are you talking about?"

"Why don't you just go tell it to your trans-phobic girlfriend?"

"What? Who? You mean Jessie? First of all we're not together anymore and second of all she's not transphobic."

"Right. My bad. See that's my problem, there's just no talking to me about these things. It's fine, you don't have to talk to me. You can just fuck off."

By now, Tucker and Alec had arrived several blocks down the street into the neighborhood, where Tucker had parked his Karmann Ghia. The top was down and Tucker made an effort to jump into the front seat without opening the door. He failed miserably, dropping his car keys and falling to the ground for an instant.

Alec grabbed the car keys off the pavement. "Come on, let me take you home."

"Fuck you, ya little pussy, you're not driving my car," Tucker replied and grabbed at Alec's arm to try and get the keys away from him.

Tucker was a full five inches taller than Alec, and though he had obviously let himself go over recent months, he had a frame that was pretty much solid muscle, so he also outweighed Alec by a goodly amount. Even so, Alec was well able to hold his own against the impaired Tucker.

Tucker began to get frustrated and swung wildly with his fist at Alec. Alec ducked, which caused Tucker to fall forward onto the pavement. Tucker, shocked by his sudden trip down, was unable to break his fall, and his face met the concrete with an unpleasant joining of flesh and rock. Alec waited and watched as Tucker rolled over onto his back to expose a face full of blood. And then, Tucker put his hands up to his face and began to weep violently.

Alec sat down on the ground with his back against the car and let Tucker cry. He offered no physical comfort, he just sat and let Tucker cry and watched the puddle of mixed blood and tears begin to form on the street. He watched the streaks of red flow down Tucker's expensive silk shirt.

It seemed like a long time passed. Several cars drove by and honked at Tucker to get out of the street. But he just lay there and cried, not saying anything. When it seemed like Tucker was having trouble breathing from all of the fluid in and on his face, Alec reached into his pocket, produced a cloth handkerchief, and threw it at Tucker's face. Tucker blew his nose and wiped the blood off of his face and slowly got up off of the ground. He didn't look at Alec at all, but instead walked around to the passenger side of the car and got in. Alec got into the driver's side and drove Tucker back to his condo. The rest of the evening Tucker spent vomiting in the bathroom and sleeping fitfully, alternately chilled to the bone or burning up, on the floor next to the toilet.

Alec called Nina to let her know that he wouldn't be coming home. He rolled up a towel for Tucker to use as a pillow and got several others out of the linen closet for him to use as blankets. He brought him a bottle of Pepto-Bismol and a glass of water, though he knew Tucker wouldn't be able to touch either for hours. Alec dimmed the light in the master bathroom and crawled into Tucker's bed, which looked as if it had not been made up for quite some time. He was too exhausted to care, though, and he quickly fell asleep.

The last year had been at turns difficult and wonderful for Alec. Alec was angry and hurt that Tucker had not been there for him through breaking up with Jesse, Smitty's death, his surgeries, and meeting Nina. He had wanted to share his ups and downs with Tucker. It was possible that Alec had grown and changed more in the last year than in the rest of his life. He was glad for the changes, but Tucker had missed it all.

For the longest time, Alec hadn't known whether to blame himself or to blame Tucker for this loss of friendship. He admired and cared for Tucker so much that he had a hard time holding Tucker responsible. But as time passed, Alec realized that he had done nothing wrong, so he had no other conclusion to draw other than to be mad at Tucker.

It had never occurred to Alec that Tucker was going through his own worst year of his life. Alec knew that Tucker was a heavy drinker, but he had never really realized how deeply that issue ran in Tucker's blood. He had never seen Tucker out of control the way he was that night. Returning to the condo and seeing the piles of dishes undone in the sink, the dirty clothes strewn throughout the house, and the empty pizza boxes, it became apparent that things had not been going well for Tucker for a while. He wasn't sure what had happened, but the man that he saw weeping in a puddle of his own blood in the street was not the confident, proud man that he had met almost a year ago. Suddenly Alec realized that he had to set aside his own feelings of hurt and anger. He realized that Tucker needed someone and it was up to him to be that someone.

Chapter 39

Though Tucker's secret decline was now apparent to Alec, it wasn't as if Tucker would suddenly learn how to accept help from someone easily. Tucker had always prided himself on nothing if not his self-sufficiency. But having been out of work for months and having progressed to the point that his major activity of the day was getting drunk, even Tucker was forced to realize that he had come very close to rock bottom, and that he needed help to reverse the trend.

Alec stayed at Tucker's house for over a week, helping Tucker clean up the mess and watching movies with him in the evenings to give him something to do besides drink. Alec called and got a referral for a substance abuse counselor for Tucker from Dr. Taffe, who Alec was only seeing a few times a year now. Alec took off of work to drive Tucker personally to the appointment.

Tucker took on an air of resigned acceptance regarding Alec's care. The two of them never talked about the life saving care that Alec was providing to Tucker. They also never talked about Tucker's problems. They just slowly, quietly, began to rebuild their trust and love for each other.

Nina seemed to support Alec's assistance of Tucker without question, even though it meant that she didn't see much of Alec for a while, and when she did see him, he was emotionally spent. Eventually, Nina began to join Alec on some of his visits with Tucker. As Nina became a part of Tucker's life, he began to see Alec as a more complete person than he ever had allowed himself to do before.

Tucker's therapist, knowing Tucker's predisposition for natural remedies, put him on Joan Mathews Larson's *Seven Weeks to Sobriety* program. The premise of the program was that alcoholism can be cured through nutrition. The program required Tucker to set a schedule for himself for taking a series of nutritional supplements, and the structure as much as the vitamins helped him to rejoin the world of the living. He began to return to his two-hour daily workout sessions and to take an interest again in his own health. He started going to his doctor again for his regular check-ups, even though he knew that his liver function was probably hovering dangerously at the level that might force him to have to go off of his testosterone. Luckily, his natural healing detox program allowed him to remain on his hormones.

In addition to one-on-one therapy and the natural healing program, Tucker also attended *SMART (Self Management And Recovery Training)* group meetings. The secular group, which differed from the typical 12-step program, taught self-empowerment and self-reliance and gave techniques for recovery and self-directed change.

Tucker's recovery wasn't without its ups and downs. But for the first time in his life, he didn't have a relapse. Tucker had been considering stopping drinking for years, but he could never think of a good enough reason. Alcohol had been a long and steady friend to Tucker, an ally through thick and thin. Alcohol was there to bring him up when he felt down, or to mellow him out when he felt uptight. Alcohol gave him courage when he needed it and helped him forget when he couldn't bear to face reality.

Tucker finally realized, though, that no matter how much he drank, things never really got any better. His jobs always managed to go south. His sexual escapades never led to anything meaningful. His friendships were only as deep as his pocket to buy the next round.

Tucker had discovered, late one night at the end of a bottle, that the only people that he truly loved were his mother, Doug, and Alec. He didn't want to know that he loved them, because he had lost all three of them. And so he realized that his life was empty. The way that he had been doing things for years and years had not brought him any closer to happiness.

He thought that maybe it was time to try doing things a different way. The only way that he could accomplish that would be never to drink again. Once he made that decision, it was only a matter of living one day after the other and not being afraid to face whatever happened, whether unpleasant or wonderful.

As Tucker got his life back on track, he began to think about what he should do about his career. Tucker had long ago learned to live his life with the best of everything: the nicest condo, the best car, and the nicest vacations. The truth was, though, now that he had covered the cost of all of the surgeries that he cared to have, he really had more money than he knew what to do with. Nina and Alec helped Tucker realize that he could live just as well with less, and thus be able to take a job based on how happy it made him instead of how much money it brought him. Alec and Nina encouraged Tucker to seek out a new career, one in which he might feel more fulfilled and accepted.

Nina had plenty of connections in the FTM and genderqueer community, and she started to keep an eye out for employment opportunities for Tucker. Nina knew of a MTF who was starting a new business and looking for a bookkeeper. She also found out that the University might be hiring.

The more that Tucker thought about it, though, the more he realized that what he wanted most of all was to be his own boss. He also really wanted to stay in the actuarial sciences that he loved so much. And he wanted to continue to be challenged by his job. He decided that he should start his own consulting firm.

Tucker certainly had enough experience as an actuary to start his own business. And he was handsome and suave enough to sell himself. Consulting also meant that he would work on any given project for a limited period of time, and then move on to something new, greatly reducing his potential for frustration and conflict with others.

With some regret, Tucker put his top of the line condo on the market and prepared to scale down to something half the cost, but still a really nice place to live. He used the profit from the sale to help him start his new business.

As part of his recovery process, Tucker determined to make amends to those that he had wronged in his life. He began with his mother. He wrote her a long letter explaining how sad he was that she wasn't part of his life anymore, and that he took responsibility for shutting her out of his life. He let her know that he didn't expect her to forgive him, but that, if she was interested, that he would like to try to be a respectful and loving son to her. He slipped the letter in the mail and left the matter in his mother's hands.

A few weeks later a beautifully handwritten card came to him in the mail that said simply, "I loved you as my daughter. I love you now as my son. If you are ready to love me as your mother then I am happy to let you." And so began a tentative, fumbling, but loving relationship between Tucker and his elderly mother. Slowly, as time passed, they learned more and more about each other and began to rebuild a bond long dead gone.

Tucker could never repay Alec, but he would try to do so little by little for the rest of his days. That left only Doug.

Tucker knew that he cared deeply about Doug, but his feelings confused him. In truth, the only wrong that he had done Doug was the neglect of friends separated by distance and different lives. But he longed to reconnect with Doug.

Tucker began to realize that his feelings for Doug might be deeper than friendship. There was too much change in Tucker's life, though. Too many things were precarious. He was opening up to too many emotions and too many relationships. Everything, every experience, was sharp and biting, like the crisp Chicago winter air. It was too much to consider that everything that he thought about his sexuality over the last twenty plus years had been wrong. It was too much to consider that he might actually be a gay man. A gay man in love with his straight best friend from college. And so he set this thought aside. And he also set aside his thoughts of reconnecting with Doug. It seemed better to Tucker to lose Doug through neglect than through conscious action.

Chapter 40

Once Tucker started to get back on track, Alec slowly began to focus on his own life again. Honestly, it had been a relief to focus on Tucker's needs for a while, after focusing for so long on his own transition.

Nina had really been outstanding throughout the episode with Tucker. She managed to give Alec the space that he needed to help and be with Tucker, but still to be around to support Alec too. And Nina had also become part of Alec's friendship with Tucker, something that no one else had ever managed to do.

Alec began to think about his life and his next steps, and he was continually amazed at how wonderful Nina was and how much he loved her. It had never occurred to Alec before that he might actually find someone to spend the rest of his life with. It had never occurred to Alec that one day he might find a wife. Alec decided that it was time to make plans to propose to Nina.

Gay marriage wasn't legal in Illinois, though the trend seemed to be slowly sweeping the US and Canada. Of course, gay marriage wasn't really the issue that Alec needed to concern himself with. What Alec needed to concern himself with was *heterosexual* marriage. It took Alec a fairly long time to get comfortable with the concept that he could, indeed, legally wed Nina because he was indeed, really a man now. As this conclusion settled in with Alec, it made him realize how far he had come in life, and also how very far he had to go, both in the world and within himself.

At one time in Illinois it had been fairly easy to get one's gender changed legally, but in recent years the process had become more complex. However, since Alec had had a hysterectomy, it was fairly easy for him to get the proper certifications from his doctors in order to get the gender on his driver's license and birth certificate changed. He felt bad for guys who had not had surgery yet, and for whom things might be more complicated.

Alec sort of wanted to complete his surgeries before proposing to Nina, so that she would know exactly what she was getting into, but since he was still paying for his chest surgery, he didn't think that he would be able to afford genital reconstruction for several years AND be able to afford an engagement ring. And he couldn't wait that long to propose. After weighing his options, Alec had decided that he wanted to have metoidioplasty, the surgery that alters the clitoris into a "micropenis" and testicular implants. He thought that this process would provide the best combination of form and function. And the metoidioplasty wouldn't rule out additional surgery if he ever decided that he wanted a more substantial penis.

Nina had already shown Alec that his clitoris could provide excellent sexual satisfaction for both of them and that she considered it the same as a penis. For the first time in his life, Alec was able to receive sexual pleasure from being touched by someone. When Nina made love to Alec, it made him feel more masculine, and this was extraordinary. If the surgery went well, metoidioplasty and implants would not only provide additional masculine visual cues, but also allow Alec to urinate standing up. And it would also allow him to have more effective and fulfilling penetrative sex, though certainly not the dramatic penetration that phalloplasty would have provided. Alec did pretty well with just his testosterone-enhanced clitoris, though, so he thought that surgery could only improve the situation.

But his finances would mean that bottom surgery would have to wait.

Alec knew that tradition dictated that one should spend three months salary on an engagement ring. But that was a hefty sum. Instead, he looked for the most beautiful thing that he could find on ONE month's salary, which was still a stretch. It took a good long time to save the money, but he did. The money mostly came out of his surgery fund. But Nina was worth it.

He put on his best suit one day and went down to Michigan Avenue to pick out the ring. He thought about bringing Jessie or Tucker along for advice, but then decided that it would be better if he made the selection on his own. He thought that there was something particularly special about buying a diamond ring for the woman that you love, something traditional and very masculine. And solitary.

Alec wanted his proposal to Nina to blow her away. He wasn't rich in terms of money, so he couldn't take her away to Paris and propose on the top of the Eiffel Tower, but he was rich in love. Nina had given Alec things that he never thought he would have: love, acceptance, and normalcy. She completed his life in a way he never thought possible. She was the most amazing woman that he had ever met. He wanted to do his best to show Nina how much he cared for her. He racked his brain, but for the longest time he couldn't think of an appropriately romantic setting for the proposal.

Jessie had often told Alec about how much she loved Madison, Wisconsin, the town in which she went to college. Alec had always wanted to visit there, but had never gotten around to it. One day he was reading the travel section of the *Chicago Tribune* and saw that there was a butterfly exhibit coming to Madison, Wisconsin where you could walk through a botanical garden with thousands of butterflies flying all around you. The idea of it was fantastically romantic. And so he began collecting information for a trip to Madison from Jessie.

Alec rented the cheapest car that he could get, a little tin can of a thing, and he and Nina headed up to Madison one Saturday morning in the late spring. Alec didn't tell Nina about the butterfly exhibit, but instead said that he just wanted to visit the town that Jessie had told him so much about.

They got to town early enough to catch the tail end of the Farmer's Market on the Capitol Square and spent the early afternoon walking up and down State Street, the downtown shopping district and pedestrian mall that connected the State Capitol building to the University of Wisconsin campus.

Late in the afternoon, Alec told Nina that he had something that he wanted to show her, and they got into the car. He drove to the near east side of town to Olbrich Botanical Gardens, where the butterfly exhibit was showing.

Nina could see by the signs at the facility that there was a butterfly exhibit, but Alec didn't think that Nina had any idea what they were in for. As the two of them entered the main interior garden exhibit they were surrounded by butterflies of all shapes, colors, and sizes. Nina gasped in glee.

"Alec, this is beautiful!"

Alec smiled proudly. Nina's reaction was right on the mark.

They wound through the gardens, pausing to look at the various butterflies as they would land on nearby tree branches or plants. Every so often, one would land on their clothing.

Alec's heart was pounding hard. He couldn't stop smiling. The setting was perfect. He was nervous and happy. He watched Nina walking amongst the butterflies and he thought that she was the most beautiful woman that he had ever seen.

After slowly winding through the exhibit for awhile, they arrived at a corner of the room that was slightly less inhabited by other spectators and Alec figured that it was his big chance.

"Nina?"

Nina turned around from where she was watching a monarch alight on a leaf. "Yes, sweetie?"

Alec reached out his hands and took Nina's and pulled her close to him. He looked directly into her eyes. "Nina, from the first moment that I met you I felt that you were different from every other woman that I had ever met in my life. I felt comfortable with you in a way that I have never felt around another person. You seemed to understand me and value the things in me that are unique and different. You opened up your life and let me love you even though I was still learning to be myself, still learning to be a man."

"Oh sweetie…" Nina started.

"Wait!" Alec said, "There's more."

Alec reached into the pocket of his shorts and pulled out a small felt covered box.

Nina put her hand over her mouth and took a deep breath.

"Nina," Alec said as he opened the box and got down on one knee, "will you make me the happiest man in the world and do me the honor of being my wife."

Nina smiled broadly and grabbed at Alec's shoulders to pull him up off of the ground. She hugged him tight and kissed him on the lips. "I love you so much, sweetie. Yes, yes definitely I will marry you." Then she kissed him again and hugged him tightly again.

Alec wanted to take Nina to a big fancy restaurant to celebrate, but he was limited by budget. They settled on a moderately priced, but atmospheric, dinner at Natt Spil, a dark downtown eatery. They told the waiter that they had just gotten engaged and scored a table in "the opium den". They drank mojitos and stared into each other's eyes over dinner.

After dinner the two of them walked the few blocks down the street to the roof of the Monona Terrace Convention Center and alternated looking out over Lake Monona in front of them and the brilliantly lit State Capitol building behind them. They chatted easily about life's daily occurrences, gazing at the stars until the moon began to rise brightly and drown out everything else in the sky. The moon reflected off of the lake and off of Nina's green eyes as Alec looked at her. Alec thought that, quite possibly he was the luckiest person in the entire world. He thought, for the first time ever, that all of the trouble and heartache in his life had been worth it to get to this moment.

After a long while, the two of them headed back to the downtown Howard Johnson's, the fanciest accommodations that Alec could manage. Alec was a bit embarrassed that it was only a few steps above the hostel that he would have normally stayed at, but Nina didn't seem to notice.

Nina's love had helped Alec learn to trust himself. She had also helped him learn to be more comfortable in his skin, surgery or no surgery. Nina really seemed to enjoy helping him learn how to appreciate his own body the way that she appreciated it.

The two of them made love that night in the most loving and gentle way, and they both fell asleep completely happy.

Chapter 41

It was a short engagement. They decided to get married a few weeks before Nina's courses started again for the fall session and to take a modest honeymoon to the Michigan coast of the lake. Money was tight for both Alec and Nina, and there were no family expectations of a huge guest list, so there was no need to plan out an elaborate affair. Nina's father did kick in a little bit of money to help pay for things, and Gail and Tucker helped out here and there with various expenses too.

Tucker insisted that Alec have a "proper" traditional bachelor party. The idea was floated early on that the bride and her attendant be allowed to tag along to the bachelor party. But Tucker would have none of that. A bachelor party was one of the last bastions of unapologetic male revelry. Tucker had served as Doug's best man a few years back, but that had been in Boston, a town that Tucker did not know well. Tucker knew every seedy inch of Chicago, though. And he knew the class joints from the holes. The girls knew that there was no way to stop Tucker from going all out, and that the only women who would be allowed would be getting paid to be naked.

Tucker assembled a small cast of characters from Alec's work, the FTM group, and from Nina's circle of FTM friends and he rented hotel rooms at the House of Blues Hotel for the whole lot of them. After check-in, the party had dinner at Meritage Cafe and Wine Bar, an upscale restaurant on North Damen Avenue. Though he was sober now, he assured that no one else at the party would be picking up the tab at each of the three bars that the crew stopped at on their way to the strip club. Tucker let the other guys get shit-faced, but assured that Alec paced himself, because he wanted him to enjoy the evening's highlights. The Hummer-limo that Tucker had reserved assured that no one would have to worry with driving that night or using the train.

At 10:20pm they stumbled into Scarlett's. Alec had never been to a strip club before, and, in fact, he didn't even know that clubs that had full nudity existed. A circular stage thrust out into the room, ringed by a brass rail and chairs. The rest of the main floor was set up with circular tables and booths. A large rectangular bar perched over the scene with a DJ booth and announcer at the back of the room. Off to the left there was a low wall of glass bricks, about 4 feet high, enclosing a separate area. Tucker had reserved the glass-enclosed VIP area for the party participants. Inside, there were several couches and big comfy chairs, and a small stage with its own lights.

The rowdy group, emboldened by their overindulgence, quickly let the strippers know who the bachelor was. One of the strippers, a young Asian woman, pulled Alec up onto the stage. She and her coworkers rubbed themselves on Alec, pressed his face into their cleavage, and shook their naked asses inches from his eyes. And then, they disappeared behind a curtain, leaving Alec on stage alone. Alec climbed down and his posse laughed and slapped him on the back. Alec couldn't help but feel more embarrassed than titillated.

Not long after that portion of the show ended, Tucker emerged with a beautiful woman on his arm. During the show Tucker had left Alec to the care of the boys and had headed off to find private entertainment for Alec. He was careful with his selection. He found a woman in her late 20s who was pretty in a simple, unpretentious way.

"Gentlemen, this is Candy," Tucker announced.

Alec rolled his eyes. *Of course her name would be Candy.*

Tucker handed Candy over to Alec and the two of them disappeared behind a door. Candy sat down in Alec's lap facing him and put her arms around his neck.

"What's your pleasure, cowboy?" Candy said.

Alec laughed nervously. He seemed uncomfortable and a little embarrassed. "I know that my friend probably paid you a great deal of money, but I'd really rather not do anything."

Candy ground her hips into Alec's crotch a little bit. "Are you sure about that?"

"Yeah. I'm really very much in love with someone. No offense."

Candy shrugged her shoulders to dismiss Alec's concern.

Alec continued, "I know that you'd probably rather not talk about personal things, but I find it fascinating that women make their living this way. Does it just feel like any other kind of job to you?"

"Do you really want to talk about this? I mean, it kind of ruins the mood," Candy said, pressing her hips against Alec's lap again.

"Yeah, totally, I'm really curious."

"Well, it's a little bit dancing, a little bit theatre, and a little bit psychology. I come in to work, do my thing, make a shitload of money and go home to my kids."

"You have kids?"

"Yeah, ages 5 and 3. Since I work nights I get to spend all day with them. Then my husband takes care of them at night."

"You're married?"

"Yeah. I guess that blows the mood for sure, huh? Unless you like that sort of thing?" Candy said with a serious tone of questioning in her voice.

"No, no. I'm not a home wrecker."

"You're sweet. What's your name?"

"Alec."

"Nice to meet you Alec. I'm Jill. But don't tell anyone, we're not supposed to use our real names here."

"Nice to meet you too, Jill."

"Your fiancée is one lucky lady, Alec." With that comment, Jill leaned over and planted a firm kiss on Alec's neck, leaving a lipstick mark. "That's for your buddies. Do me a favor and tell them I blew you or something, okay?"

"Sure, no problem."

Candy deposited Alec with his friends, whose eyes were beginning to glaze over from the constant barrage of nakedness.

"Your friend was nice. Anything that I can do for you?" Candy asked Tucker.

Tucker smiled. "No, Candy, tonight is all about my friend here. Maybe some other time." He held out another twenty-dollar bill in her direction.

Candy took the twenty, shrugged her shoulders, and disappeared into the crowd.

The group stayed at the club and watched several more shows. The strippers began to gang up on Alec and act out more and more ridiculous fantasies on him, culminating in the Asian stripper removing Alec's belt, pulling down his pants, and spanking his boxer short covered bottom with his own belt.

This final performance seemed like a good capper on the evening, and so the group headed back out to the limo and back to the hotel. At the hotel, Tucker pulled Alec away from the rest of the group as they headed to the elevators to return to their rooms to sleep or vomit away the evening's sins. Tucker led Alec to the hotel bar.

"Geez, Tucker, I can't drink anymore," Alec said.

"Don't worry," Tucker said, and then he ordered them two Perriers with lime at the bar.

Tucker gathered the drinks and headed to a booth in a dark corner. Alec followed, exhausted and curious as to what Tucker was up to. They sat down together and Tucker poured his water into a glass and squeezed lime over it.

"What's this all about?" Alec asked.

Tucker looked at Alec for a long time with a half grin on his face. He looked down at the glass of water in front of him as the bubbles rose to the top and he took a deep breath and then looked Alec right in the eyes.

"You saved my life. Not once, but twice. You reminded me what it was like to have a real friend at a time when I hadn't had one for a very long time. And then, after I was a real ass to you, you came back and kept me from drinking myself into the grave." Tucker paused and looked down at his glass again. Alec was surprised by this sudden and direct honesty from Tucker.

After a moment, he looked a bewildered Alec back in the eye. "You're a good man. You're a better man than I've ever been. And I can never repay you the debt that I owe you."

Before Alec could think through the haze of over-stimulation, exhaustion, and alcohol that was clouding his mind of what to say in response, Tucker reached into the breast pocket of his coat and pulled out an envelope and handed it to Alec.

Alec opened the envelope and found a blank check with Tucker's signature on it. In the memo line in very small, precise letters it read "for Alec's bottom surgery."

Alec blinked twice and read the small writing again. He felt light headed and he didn't think it was just the booze.

"I don't understand." Alec said.

"And here I thought I was so slick about it," Tucker answered as he settled back in his seat and smiled broadly at Alec.

"This is crazy," Alec continued.

"Look," Tucker began, "I have the money and you don't. You want the surgery and I don't. And I owe you big time."

"No you don't, I mean, we're friends, I was just helping you the only way that I could."

"And this is what I can do for you. So let me do it." Tucker said and looked hard at Alec with a look that told him that the discussion was over.

Tucker thought a moment and then added, "Don't you *dare* feel guilty about this. After this, we're even. We're back to just being friends. Brothers. Nobody owes anybody anything. Understand?"

"Sure," Alec said, still in shock and disbelief, but knowing in an odd way, that this gesture allowed Tucker to regain the dignity that he had lost through his recovery. Little did Tucker know that his recovery from his alcohol dependence, and allowing his friends to help him with that, was the most dignified thing that he had ever done in his entire life.

While the boys were out carousing, the girls were having their own fun. Gail hosted an elaborate tea party for the gang in the afternoon where Nina got to open her shower gifts. In the evening, Jessie took Nina and the rest of the girls out to Club 69, where she had arranged for a special show of the Chicago Kings drag king troupe. Through special negotiation with the troupe leader Mr. Izzie Big, she had arranged for a particularly erotic performance.

Chapter 42

A week later Nina was back at Gail's house at the center of a bustle of activity. Women were attending to every corner of her body, someone fixing hair here, someone else painting nails there. A photographer was mingling amongst the flurry of activity taking candid shots.

Downtown Tucker and Alec were picking up their tuxes at the shop. They headed back to Tucker's place and began assembling their outfits. Tucker set aside the cheap fiddly-bits that came with the rented tuxes and produced a set of very classy cuff links and button covers that he had bought Alec especially for occasion.

The doorbell rang and it was Ray, Tucker's buddy the doorman from Friendly's. Ray, all-American boy that he was, owned a fabulous convertible muscle car and Tucker had gotten him to agree to loan it out for the wedding so long as Ray could chauffeur.

As luck would have it, the weather was perfect. Ray, Tucker, and

Alec headed down to the lakeshore in Ray's beautiful car. The girls drove over to Jessie's neighborhood and parked the cars and walked the few blocks to the lake.

The ceremony was simple and elegant. Nina's Unitarian minister performed the ceremony in front of about 30 of Nina's classmates, Alec's coworkers, a handful of FTM friends, and a few members of Nina's family. Nina's father and her late mother's sister had driven out from Ohio for the occasion. Nina's father gave her away. Tucker and Jessie stood up for their friends at the ceremony. One of Nina's classmates and Gail each offered readings about love and commitment.

Alec had never given much thought to the details of weddings. He thought that this wedding was particularly beautiful, though. Some people might hope for an elaborate wedding, but he was just happy to have an ordinary, simple ceremony. The most extraordinary part of the ceremony to him was how ordinary it was, in fact. He was thrilled to be just a normal guy getting married in a normal way. He was completely certain of his desire to spend his life with Nina. He kept feeling like he had to pinch himself to assure that this was really happening.

Gail had the carpentry shop cleaned up and cleared out and paid to have caterer's bring food in for the reception. They managed to squeeze the wedding party in for a standing-style mingling reception complete with a small dance floor and live music.

Tucker brought an electric keyboard and played at the reception along with an electric bass player and a drummer with a snare drum and a hi-hat cymbal. As Tucker had emerged from the haze of his alcoholism, he had taken up more than just good physical health habits, but was also trying his best to build activities to nourish his heart and soul too. He had taken up daily meditation practice and had also returned to playing the piano regularly.

One day Tucker had run into Jeff, the bass player that he had played in a jazz combo with when he had first moved to Chicago. Back in the day they were a decent group, but they hadn't played very seriously. That had been almost 20 years ago, though, and in the interim Jeff had perfected his skills and had been playing professionally off and on. When the two of them ran into each other Jeff had been out of the music game for a year or so, but seeing Tucker had piqued his interest again and the two of them started goofing around together once a week or so. It was a happy coincidence, too, that they were both recovering alcoholics, so their music together no longer involved alcohol the way that it once had. Eventually, they picked up a drummer, and the wedding was the third time that they had played out together as a group. Tucker used his connections at so many bars around Chicago to set up gigs, and the three of them, who all happily had day jobs, were content to play those shows here and there for a few extra bucks and a good time.

After several hours of chatting and eating and dancing, the crowd at the reception cleared out and Gail sent the happy couple away so that she could clean up. Ray had long since drunk himself under the table and Tucker had driven him home in the muscle car and taken a cab back to the reception. So Alec and Nina were forced to get a cab of their own, which they took to The Drake, where Tucker had gotten them a room for the wedding night.

They checked in and went up to the room and took off their wedding clothes. Nina leaned back on the bed dressed just in her panties and slip and sighed an exhausted sigh. Alec was down to his boxers, dress socks, and unbuttoned tux shirt. He walked over to the bed and sat down at Nina's feet and began rubbing them for her. He knew that she wasn't used to wearing heels and that she had been in them all day. Nina closed her eyes and enjoyed the foot massage. Alec looked at his beautiful new wife and marveled at the twists and turns that his life had taken. He had spent the entire day surrounded by people who cared about him and who wanted the best for him. It was a remarkable situation and a remarkable turnabout. He felt surrounded by love. He realized as he rubbed Nina's toes between his hands, though, that the love around him was only possible because he had finally learned how to love himself.

22053477R00132

Made in the USA
Lexington, KY
10 April 2013